THE 10 STEPS TO FINANCIAL WELLNESS

Your Personal Guide To Rock-Solid Financial Health

Jeff S. Rubleski

What Others Are Saying About *The 10 Steps To Financial Wellness...*

"From budgeting, to debt reduction and saving for retirement, *The 10 Steps To Financial Wellness* has everything you need to finally take charge of your finances. Everyone at the workplace should have this book. With special pricing for multiple copy orders, your organization can put a copy of this excellent financial wellness resource in the hands of every employee in your organization. WOW!"

— Deborah Seyler, MBA
Executive Director
Wellness Council of Wisconsin

"*The 10 Steps To Financial Wellness* is an illuminating, practical and factual must read for anyone seeking financial stability at any stage of life. The chapters that focus on employer-sponsored benefits, saving/investing and insurance are an invaluable guide for maximizing employer provided benefit programs for every working American."

— Arthur A. Fabbro, Jr.
Director Total Compensation
Magna International, Inc.

"*The 10 Steps To Financial Wellness* is filled with valuable personal finance information that will help people of all ages make solid life decisions. It's a great reference book that can be used time and time again as your life situation changes."

— Cindy Larsen
President
Muskegon Area Chamber of Commerce

"*The 10 Steps To Financial Wellness* will provide each reader with countless benefits but none more important than the actual steps to achieve long-term financial wellness. This book applies to people at every stage in life. In fact, this book will be the first graduation gift I select for each of my four children."

— Orlando L. Blanco, J.D.
Blanco, Wilczynski, P.L.L.C.

Wellness Council of America
9802 Nicholas Street, Suite 315
Omaha, NE 68114
402-827-3590
www.welcoa.org

This book can be purchased for a very reasonable price when ordering multiple copies. It is the hope of the author and publisher that organizations of all sizes will purchase a copy for each employee or key stakeholder in the organization. Contact The Wellness Council of America for pricing and shipping options.

Book Design by Adam Paige, Wellness Council of America Design Team

A portion of the proceeds are directed to the Stanley L. Rubleski Memorial Scholarship Endowment. This endowment provides annual tuition funding for a student-athlete at Hackett Catholic Central High School in Kalamazoo, Michigan.

ISBN-13: 978-0-9791490-0-9
ISBN-10: 0-9791490-0-2

Second Edition: May 2009

Printed in the U.S.A.

This book is printed on environmentally-friendly paper and using soy-based ink.

Contents

ABOUT THE AUTHOR
Jeff S. Rubleski

Jeff S. Rubleski serves as Director of Sales Strategy for Blue Cross Blue Shield of Michigan. He is an employee benefits expert, with expertise in defined contribution pension plans, healthcare financing, comprehensive employee wellness programming, consumer-directed healthcare and personal finance.

Prior to joining Blue Cross Blue Shield of Michigan over ten years ago, Jeff spent over fifteen years in the banking, health and financial publishing industries and served as the Marketing Strategist and Chief Operating Officer for the Wellness Council of America (WELCOA) in Omaha, Nebraska. During his tenure at WELCOA, Jeff introduced the *Well Workplace* health newsletter and *Just for You* health brochures that are distributed to employers and insurance carriers throughout the United States.

He earned his MBA from Grand Valley State University and serves as an adjunct faculty member in Grand Valley State University's Finance Department. He has published several nationally-circulated articles in the areas of personal finance, employee wellness programming and consumer-directed healthcare.

Jeff is an engaging speaker on a variety of personal finance, health benefits and worksite wellness topics (e-mail inquiries to: **rubleski@comcast.net**). He writes a monthly personal finance column in WELCOA's *Well Workplace* health newsletter. He has a passion for consumer education and for making complex financial matters easy to understand. Through *The 10 Steps To Financial Wellness,* Jeff will show readers how to establish a solid foundation for long-term financial wellness. It is his belief that overall personal wellness is enhanced when an individual has a sustainable plan in place to build financial net worth.

Jeff lives in Muskegon, Michigan with his wife, Betty, and his two children, Jeff and Emily.

Disclaimer

This book is written to provide accurate and authoritative information regarding the subject matter covered. *The author's insight and opinions are his own and not those of past or current employers.* It is sold with the understanding that the author and the publisher are not engaged in rendering legal, accounting, financial planning or other professional service. If legal, financial or other professional advice is required, the services of a competent professional person should be sought.

The author has made every effort to provide accurate Internet addresses and telephone numbers at the time of publication; neither the author nor the publisher assumes any responsibility for errors or other changes that occur after publication.

Every effort has been made to make this book as complete and accurate as possible. However, there may be mistakes, both typographical and in content. Therefore, the information in this book should be considered a general guide to the subject matter covered.

The purpose of this book is to educate the reader on basic personal finance principles. Neither the author nor the publisher shall have any liability or responsibility to any person or entity with respect to any loss or damage caused, or alleged to have been caused, directly or indirectly, by the information contained in this book.

Acknowledgements

I'd like to thank The Wellness Council of America (WELCOA) for its support of this book. As a leader in workplace health promotion, WELCOA recognizes the link between personal and financial wellness, and the need for employees to take the right steps to achieve financial wellness in their lives.

A special thanks to my personal finance mentor, Professor Gregg Dimkoff, Ph.D., CLU and CFP, from Grand Valley State University. Gregg had the greatest influence on my learning and passion for personal finance during my college years. I've known Gregg for over twenty-five years and he has the sharpest financial mind of anyone I've ever met. His guidance throughout this book has been invaluable.

Thank you to my family and coworkers for their encouragement and wise input on the content of this book. The many hours it took to produce this book would not have been possible without the incredible support I received from my family, especially my wife, Betty and my brother, Tony.

This book is dedicated to Betty, Jeff and Emily

Foreword

WHEN YOU FAST FORWARD 25 YEARS, I see some serious problems looming on the horizon. First, there are presently 80 million baby boomers—those born between 1946 and 1964. This is the largest population bulge in the history of the United States. It is the proverbial pig through the python. And because these baby boomers will be retiring steadily in the next 20 years, this enormous group of people is going to put a strain on how we do business in the U.S.

How so?

This brings us to our second concern—life expectancy. Through advancements in modern medicine, technology, and innovations in prevention and lifestyle modification, people in this country will be living longer...a lot longer. Right now the life expectancy in the U.S. is approximately 78 years. But through these advancements, it is likely that we will see the average life expectancy reach into the mid to upper 80s in the next 25 years. Now, put that into perspective and think about 80 million people living into their late 80s.

Which brings us to issue number three—retirement. With 80 million people living into their mid to upper 80s, it's likely that Social Security will not provide the safety net it once did. For example, decades ago there were approximately 18 people contributing to Social Security for every person that retired. Today, there are five people contributing toward the Social Security funds which will be allocated to the baby boom generation. As a result, political and economic experts predict that, unless changes are made soon, Social Security will be a forgone conclusion. This means that, without Social Security, 80 million baby boomers will now need to start saving like mad in order to provide for their retirement years—which could be as many as 25 depending on when they choose to retire.

Which logically brings us to our fourth concern—the present savings rate. Plain and simple, people in this country are not saving enough. Whether it's because of poor financial management, credit card debt, or catastrophic circumstances, it's clear that citizens of the United States are woefully unprepared for a rainy day.

And when you connect all the dots, that's why this book is so important. In one simple soft cover book, any individual from any walk of life can now get solid personal financial information which, if followed, will help them immensely not only in managing their day-to-day affairs, but preparing and thriving in retirement.

But make no mistake about it; good financial management doesn't happen by accident. It takes head knowledge, heartfelt commitment, and backbone in order to run successfully through the financial gauntlet which comprises day-to-day life.

For those who successfully incorporate the recommendations in this book, the payoffs will be substantial. Not only will you be financially prepared, but you will also lead a much healthier and less stressful existence. You'll be able to do the things you want to do and be healthy enough to enjoy every step along the way. For those who choose not to listen, well that's a horse of a different color. The beautiful part about this proposition is that it's entirely up to you.

Again, that's why I believe that this book is an important (translated essential) tool in helping you to get started. And although it's going to be a long road back for a lot of people, it can be accomplished. But you've got to start today. This book will point you in the right direction and allow you to successfully navigate the rough waters which shipwreck most people.

I congratulate you on taking this most important first step, and I wish you the very best in financial health in the years to come.

Dr. David Hunnicutt, President
Wellness Council of America

OF AMER
GOD WE TRUS
GOD WE TRUST
LIBERT

INTRODUCTION

The 10 Steps To Financial Wellness

Your Personal Guide To Rock-Solid Financial Health

By Jeff S. Rubleski

OUR PERSONAL FINANCES AND OUR OVERALL WELLNESS ARE INTERTWINED. Think about the relationships you currently have. Your personal finances have a direct impact on some of your most valued relationships. When you take proactive steps to gain control of your personal finances, you'll find that your overall wellness and personal relationships will often improve. Personal finances are a core component of most human relationships. Stress caused by a host of financial issues can wreak havoc on the relationships we value most (it's a leading cause of divorce in The United States) and can cause us to lose sight of the important things in life that money alone cannot buy.

The 10 Steps To Financial Wellness is written to appeal to those in all phases of their careers, including those just entering the workforce and those who are just a few years away from retirement. Building long-term financial wellness is an easier proposition for those who are early in their career. It's easier because those with decades before retirement have time to accumulate savings and to harness the power of compound interest to grow their investments. *However, if you are in the later stages of your career and find that you need to save quite a bit more to have a secure retirement, don't despair. You have options.* The good news is that we are living longer and healthier lives than our parents' generation. This means that most of us can choose to work longer than our parents and still enjoy a long and hopefully healthful retirement. Also remember that the traditional notion of retirement is rapidly changing. Earning just a modest income doing meaningful part-time work in retirement can go a long way in helping you to have a financially secure and an emotionally fulfilling retirement. There are many ways to build long-term financial wellness and this book will provide the roadmap through easy to follow chapter Steps to help you in this journey.

This book will help you to take actionable steps to improve your overall financial wellness, which is the foundation for building long-term financial independence. *And the best part of the journey to building financial wellness is that you don't need to earn a six-figure salary or have a million dollar retirement fund to experience the benefits of financial wellness in your life.* You also don't need an advanced business or professional degree to understand what it takes to build a rock-solid financial foundation.

What's needed to attain long-term financial wellness is practical guidance to help you avoid costly financial mistakes and some common sense advice on how to take advantage of the opportunities you have to build a secure financial future. By taking proactive steps in the process of building your personal financial foundation, you'll experience a sense of liberation from the stress that financial issues can present in your life. You'll gain perspective and you'll also develop confidence in your ability to make positive, liberating changes in your life through a proactive approach to managing your career and your personal finances.

By embracing the time-tested principles in each chapter Step of this book, you'll be prepared to focus your energies on your top priorities in a proactive manner. You'll also give yourself a great opportunity to achieve financial independence through making wise decisions with your hard-earned money and by taking full advantage of the benefits your employer offers.

So let's get started on our journey together in pursuit of financial wellness for you and for those who may depend on you…

STEP 1
Review Your Current Financial Situation

"To secure a solid financial future, you must know the condition of your finances today and make a plan for tomorrow."

IF SOMEONE YOU TRUSTED SAID TO YOU: *"Please tell me how much you owe and also tell me the value of what you own,"* would you know the answer? Most people either don't know the answer to this question or are unable to provide an accurate response because they don't know the amount of debt they have and they don't know the value of the assets they possess. To complete **Step 1** in your journey to financial wellness, it's essential for you to know the answer to this question. When you know how much you owe and the value of what you own, you'll have the two necessary ingredients for building financial wellness—it's called your personal financial net worth.

What's Your Financial Net Worth?

In a given year, most people will spend more time planning a vacation than they will examining their daily spending decisions. Why? I believe that most people just don't know where to start when planning their finances.

A Personal Financial Net Worth Statement can be found in **Appendix 1-1** (located in the Appendix Section in the back of the book). Completing this Statement will allow you to find out your net worth. Caution: you might find this exercise to be a sobering experience! My experience with people of all ages has taught me that most people find that the debts they owe are much more than they estimated and the value of what they own is less than anticipated. In fact in a study released January 6, 2006 by the Consumer Federation of America and the Financial Planning Association, 49 percent of Americans don't know how to estimate their net worth.[1] **Appendix 1-1** will provide the format you'll need to calculate your financial net worth. Take the time to complete this step, as it will serve as a key benchmark in your journey toward financial wellness.

Whatever your financial "net worth" happens to be on the last line of **Appendix 1-1**, understand that what you've accomplished puts you in a special category of people. Most people simply don't take the time or just don't know where to begin in pulling together the necessary information to determine their overall net worth. By completing this exercise, you've taken a giant step in your journey toward attaining financial wellness. The significance of knowing your current net worth is that it will give you a critical "baseline" from which you can measure annual progress in measuring a hopefully growing financial net worth.

The median net worth of all U.S. households (half the households had less) was $93,100 in 2004.[2] When a median value is used, half of the households had less net worth and half had more. The most affluent 10% of U.S. households had a median net worth of $1,430,000. Note that these median net worth estimates include the equity amount in homes owned and the value of retirement accounts. Taking a closer look at net worth, **Exhibit 1-1** shows median net worth by age. **Exhibit 1-2** charts median net worth by the level of household income. The extensive analysis of household net worth is conducted by the Federal Reserve every three years. Since 1995, family net worth has increased at an annual rate of about 2.5%. Assuming this growth rate in annual net worth continues at annual growth rate of 2.5%, median net worth for U.S. households in 2009 should be around $105,334.

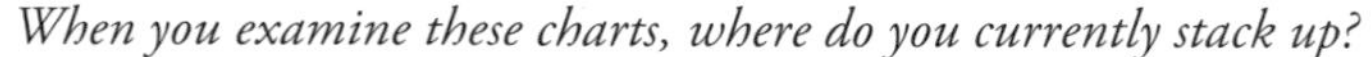

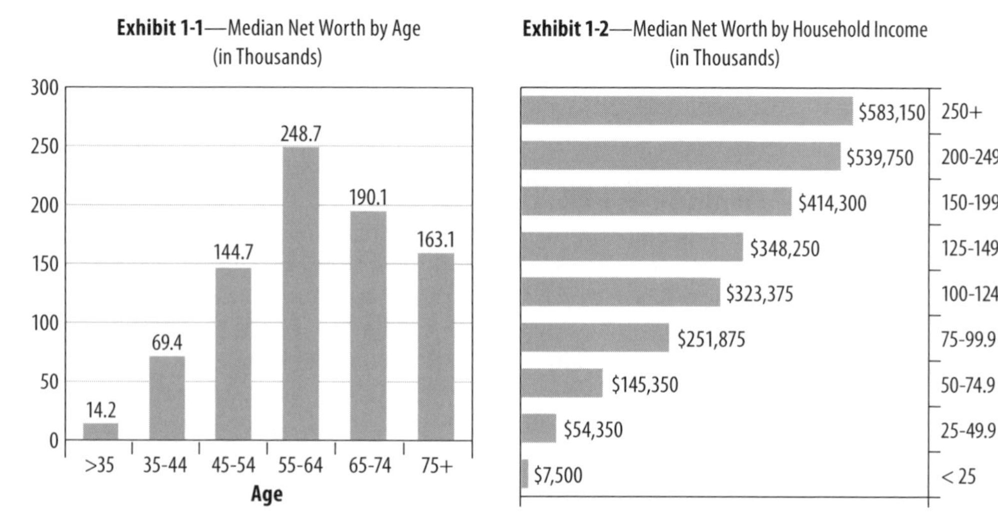

Track Financial Net Worth Progress Annually

Appendix 1-1 provides you with the simple steps necessary to determine your financial net worth. For those of you who are spreadsheet savvy, you may wish to place this on a spreadsheet for ease of updating in future periods. For most people, I recommend examining financial net worth on an annual basis. I always compare my financial net worth progress on January 1 of each year. I have a hanging file established for this and I've been tracking my progress since 1986. It's really inspirational and motivating for me to look at how my financial net worth has grown since then. After completing my net worth statement on January 1, I set a goal for where I want my net worth to be in the following year and I write it down. When the following year comes, I compare my goal to my actual financial net worth for the year. By listing my goal for the upcoming year, I've found that it serves to give me an overall direction for the year and helps me in my routine assessment of spending and investing throughout the year.

Examine Your Monthly Cash Flow

Cash flow is either positive or negative over a period of time. That's why it's important to draft a monthly budget, or as I call it, a monthly cash flow statement. **Appendix 1-2** (located in the Appendix Section in the back of the book) is a sample *Monthly Cash Flow/Budget Statement* that you can use to find out whether you are generating positive or negative cash flow each month. It takes positive cash flow to build your financial net worth. If you find that your monthly cash flow is negative, or that it is not high enough to reach your savings and investment goals, take a good look at your discretionary spending. These areas include expenses where you have considerable control including dining out, entertainment, transportation choices and clothing. It's these "discretionary" spending areas that are often the easiest to find additional cash flow to apply to your long-term saving or investing goals. It takes a measure of discipline to get discretionary spending items under control and your monthly cash flow statement will help you to pinpoint discretionary spending patterns.

Make sure that you work with members of your household to get both understanding and agreement on the spending adjustments that will be necessary to build your monthly cash flow statement and your net worth. This requires discipline and ongoing communication. Set a goal for your cash flow each month and take the time to monitor your results at the conclusion of each month. If your income and expenses fluctuate or if you feel that monthly evaluation might be too tedious, commit to at least a quarterly evaluation. If it's the first time you've ever looked at your income and expenses, you should commit to at least 4 months of budgeting before going to a quarterly evaluation period. You simply need to know your overall cash flow patterns over a consistent period of time to build financial wellness. Your monthly cash flow has a direct impact on your financial net worth. Listed below is how your monthly cash flow will impact your overall financial net worth:

The Monthly Cash Flow/Financial Net Worth Statement Connection:

Monthly cash flow impacts your net worth statement. Without ongoing positive cash flow, the growth of your financial worth over the long run will be compromised. Consistent, positive monthly cash flow is a requisite to building your financial net worth.

Keep Good Records—Get a Filing Cabinet and a Shredder

A file cabinet for your financial matters is essential. If you don't have one, get one and devote it to organizing your personal finances. This is a must for keeping good, organized records. A well-organized file cabinet will allow you to keep key financial documents, bills, statements, etc. located in one place for easy reference.

Let's start with how you pay your bills each month. What does your filing system look like? Do you have one? Step one in this area is to set up a bill paying system. The best part here is that it's very easy to set up a system for bill paying.

Here's what I've been doing for the past twenty five years. I have two hanging folders established for bill paying. One file is for bills due in the middle of the month, the second file is for bills due at the end of the month. When my bills trickle in each month, they are immediately placed in the appropriate file. I then pay the vast majority of my bills just twice a month by pulling the appropriate file and paying all the bills in the file. It's simple, easy to remember and keeps me organized. (Hey, it's "low-tech," but it works!)

To minimize clutter, I shred the previous invoice when a new invoice arrives, reflecting my previous month's payment. Also establish hanging files for current year income tax items needed for your income taxes. If you itemize your taxes, you might want to set up subfolders to keep track of receipts or important documents, if needed. By setting up hanging folders for key financial documents, you'll be in position to quickly locate appropriate financial documents when needed. You'll also save hours in finding key documents for annual income tax preparation.

Keep the Identity Thieves Away!

Identity theft is a byproduct of the information age we live in. Buy a shredder and use it to shred documents that contain personal information such as your name, Social Security Number, account numbers, passwords, account balances, etc. You can find a good home shredder for under $50 at an office supply store or on the Internet. Most identity theft occurs due to careless personal disposal of sensitive financial documents. By shredding your personal and financial documents, you'll go a long way to protecting your identity and your personal credit.

With more of us using our personal computers to access banking accounts, financial accounts and to make online purchases, securing your PC from online thieves is crucial. Invest in a comprehensive software security package that includes a "firewall" to protect your PC from "cyber-hacking" from unauthorized sources. There are a number of excellent software security packages available for purchase. Two of the leading companies in this area are Symantec, www.symantec.com and McAfee, www.mcafee.com. After loading the most recently updated software security package on your PC, make sure that you also download periodic updates as soon as they are available. Cyber-thieves work non-stop and software security packages need to be periodically updated to ensure that your PC has the latest protection from the latest virus that can wreak havoc on your software files or compromise your sensitive financial information. Plan to invest $50 to $100 per year on PC security software. This can be one of the best investments you can make to protect your software files and financial information from cyber-theft.

Financial Wellness—Making the Complex Simple

I believe that there is a true need to help people deal with their personal finances in a proactive, understandable way that improves their overall wellness. Yes, there is a considerable amount of financial information available to you. To make good financial decisions you must possess a solid financial foundation and develop a mindset that will allow you to make consistently good financial decisions. Understand that you'll continue to make financial mistakes. But when you have a solid financial foundation and you are consistently building and tracking your financial net worth, you'll position yourself to minimize your financial mistakes and maximize your financial opportunities. You'll develop a proactive versus a reactive mindset when it comes to your personal finances. You'll steadily take the necessary steps to attain financial wellness in your life.

Financial Literacy—It's Up to You

Think about the formal education you've had. Whether you completed high school or have earned an advanced higher education degree, chances are your educational training didn't address what you need to know about personal finance. Unfortunately our schools do not prepare us for the financial decisions we need to make when we enter the workforce. Most of us learn about personal finance through trial and error. Financial mistakes are often costly and can take years to erase. Look how easy it is to get a credit card. The credit card companies use a variety of sophisticated marketing methods to determine the best "prospects" for their cards. It's no secret that their best customers use other credit cards generously and typically carry a balance each month. They often extend outrageous lines of credit to people who simply should not incur another dime of debt!

I'll have more to say about credit card debt in Step #4. *The overuse of credit cards is the number one challenge many people have.* If you routinely carry credit card balances you must make elimination of these balances a top priority. If you don't get control of credit card debt, you will more than likely fail to build financial wellness for yourself and your family.

The Financial Wellness Connection

One of my goals in writing this book is to give you the foundational steps to allow you to stay well ahead of the median net worth benchmark for your age group and your income level. Don't despair if you are below the median benchmark for your age group or income level at this point. Remember, it's how you finish the journey toward long-term financial wellness that counts. By making the right spending, saving and investing decisions, you'll position yourself to gain any lost ground and to build the discipline to stay ahead of the pack when it comes to growing your financial net worth.

A key issue in measuring personal wellness involves how we react to the daily stress in our lives. Stress is a fact of life. We need it to live. In just the right amount it is actually good for us. It motivates us to take action and often gives us a purpose for our actions. But the "dark side" of stress is *distress.* Having too much stress in our lives has a compounding effect that, left unchecked, ultimately becomes distress.

Take a look at what causes you stress, and if you're like a majority of people, the causes of the stress often have a direct link to financial issues or decisions you've made in your life. When you think about the stress you've encountered in personal and family relationships, there is more than likely some financial component behind the strained relationships. Wellness means different things to different people. Many people believe that wellness is achieved when a person has optimal health. Others may say that wellness is truly a state of mind.

Since individual wellness is a personal issue, what are the key components that will lead to overall personal wellness? I believe that there are three key factors that drive overall personal wellness. Following is a definition of personal wellness based on my 20-plus years of experience and research within the health, wellness and financial professions:

Definition of Personal Wellness

Three key factors drive personal wellness. **First**, the individual needs to have, or is striving to attain, good physical and mental health through appropriate lifestyle decisions. **Second**, the individual's spiritual side or deep connection to others or noble causes is developed. ***Third**, the individual demonstrates a level of control over the material needs of life through careful ongoing decisions involving personal finances and the development of financial wellness.*

The first two listed components from the definition are familiar. Some experts refer to these first two components as fulfilling the mind, body and spirit connection to wellness. I've added the component of financial wellness to this definition. I've added this third component to this definition because your personal finances have a direct impact on the mind, body and spirit components of overall personal wellness. Having step three in place serves to leverage the first two components of the Personal Wellness Definition.

Most current wellness programming is directed to improving our overall physical and mental health, the first component that describes personal wellness. Examples impacting the first component of wellness include lifestyle decisions regarding diet, nutrition, stress management, exercise and health screenings, such as annual physical examinations. The second component is a sensitive one for some people. It's often referred to as the "spiritual side" of wellness. If you consider yourself a spiritual person then this component will likely make sense to you. But, if you don't consider yourself overly spiritual, or your downright non-spiritual, there's room in this definition for you also. If you have a favorite charity or activity that helps others or improves your community in some way then you do have a passion or a "calling" for something beyond yourself. This second area of wellness will help you to find lifelong meaning and is essential for a fulfilling life. *The third area, the development of personal financial wellness is where this book will focus.*

On the next page and at the conclusion of each chapter Step, you'll find an *Action Step Checklist*. Take the time to review each Checklist to ensure that you understand and implement the key concepts outlined in the chapter Step.

Once you've completed your *Action Step Checklist*, go to **Step #2**, where I will share practical ideas you can use to develop yourself and your career options…

1

ACTION STEP CHECKLIST

Step #1 Action Step Checklist

The Action Step Checklist will help you to implement some of the key concepts mentioned in this chapter. When you've finished the Action Step, place a ✓ next to the Step to document your progress.

Here is your Action Step Checklist from Step #1:

- ______Complete the personal **Financial Net Worth Statement** located in the Appendix Section of this book.

- ______Prepare your **Monthly Cash Flow (budget) Statement** located in the Appendix Section of this book.

- ______Monitor your Monthly Cash Flow progress each month with members of your household (if applicable) to ensure understanding of spending decisions and to build agreement on adjustments that may need to be made to keep your budget on track.

- ______Assess your current health status. Make exercise a part of your lifestyle and commit to eating a balanced diet and get enough rest. If you are out of shape or have health issues, work with your family physician to develop a plan to improve your overall health. Optimal health is a key component to long-term financial wellness.

- ______Write down your long-term goals and what is important to you. Are there special causes or spiritual endeavors that matter to you? Identifying the important goals in your life will help you to stay focused while you are building financial wellness.

- ______Review your filing system for bill paying and maintenance of personal financial statements. Take the necessary steps to secure a filing cabinet for your key financial items and establish a system for filing and bill paying.

- ______Buy a document shredder to properly dispose of financial or health documents that contain personal information. A leading cause of identity theft is careless disposal of sensitive personal documents.

- ______Invest in a comprehensive software security package that includes a "firewall" to protect your personal information and software files from viruses and "cyber-theft." Be sure to keep your software security package updated to protect your PC from the latest "cyber-threats."

STEP 2
Develop Yourself And Your Career Options Will Follow

"Find a job you love and you'll never work another day in your life."

Are You Prepared To Thrive In A Global Economy?

Global competition has had an impact on all of us. The benefits of "globalization" include better quality and more product choices for consumers at lower prices. Just think about how globalization has reduced the cost of every day items such as television sets, personal computers and digital electronic devices. These cost savings allow us to buy more products for less money, often with improved quality. Sound too good to be true? The answer is a resounding YES if your job has been adversely impacted by global competition. Over the past decade, scores of U.S. manufacturing jobs have been lost to global competitors. Like it or not, globalization will continue to accelerate in the future. So how do you thrive in this unsettling, ever-changing, globalized economy? *One way to stay ahead is to continually make an investment in your skills and assess the careers or vocations that will be in demand in the future.*

Accept the fact that your current job skills could become totally obsolete in a matter of just a few years! If you think that this only relates to manufacturing jobs, *think again*. The global economy continues to transform and will impact every industry and profession, as employers look to secure the best worldwide talent and resources at the best price. The key to career success involves keeping your skills razor-sharp in your current industry and developing skills that can be transferred into other industries. Those who demonstrate flexibility and the ability to adapt quickly to changing circumstances will establish the necessary skills to thrive in our rapidly changing, globalized economy.

Good Fortune Comes To Those Who Are Prepared

Have you ever noticed that some people seem to be blessed with quite a bit of luck, good fortune, impeccable timing, etc. when it comes to their job or career? Sometimes each of us happens to be in the right place at the right time when something good happens. But, when you look beyond the surface of those who seem to get all the breaks in a job or career, you'll often find one common denominator: *preparation.*

Henry Ford is revered for his ingenuity in devising mass production methods to make automobiles plentiful and affordable for the average worker. Some people thought he was a genius and many in his time marveled at his stunning business success. But Mr. Ford made an insightful and now famous quote about his inventions that led to his business success. He said: *"Innovation is 99 percent perspiration and one percent inspiration."* What he was really saying is that hard work and preparation are the fundamental ingredients for success. Mr. Ford didn't just fall into his good fortune. He worked at it, failed often, but managed to keep his focus on the task at hand. His success allowed him to achieve his vision of making automobiles affordable for the working class.

Develop A Proactive Career Mindset

The world is full of "underachievers." These are people who seem to have all the right training, education and personal qualities to succeed, but they fail to achieve their full potential. Then there are the "overachievers." They seem to achieve great career and life outcomes, sometimes with limited skills. The overachievers often seem to follow the path that Mr. Ford credited for his success. Most overachievers follow the proactive mindset when it comes to career and personal development.

People are complex and we all possess unique talents and skills. There is a career mindset that I've observed in people over my twenty five-plus years in the business world. People generally fall into two career mindsets. The first is what I call the "passive" career mindset and the second is the "proactive" career mindset. Which camp are you in? To help you decide, here are my definitions of the two mindsets:

- **Passive Career Mindset:** The individual is employed in a job or career that meets the individual's career and financial needs. There is limited effort devoted to "personal development" and acquiring the skills to have a back up plan should something go wrong with the individual's current job or career. These individuals often "play it safe" at work and are afraid to take prudent risks that can advance their career. They often view themselves as victims of circumstances when something goes wrong.

- **Proactive Career Mindset:** The individual makes personal development through additional training, education, credentials, etc. a key priority throughout his/her career. Career challenges are viewed as opportunities to learn and they aren't afraid to fail. These individuals are "lifelong learners." They're in-tune with the ever-changing economy and are willing to make the necessary personal and career changes to keep ahead in the changing economic environment. These individuals take personal responsibility for their personal and career development and bounce back quickly from mistakes or setbacks.

Personal Observations On The Power Of Mindset

I've observed that most people fall into the passive career mindset. Why? I think that people tend to get comfortable with their work situation and the "predictability" it tends to provide to all of us. Although doing a good job does give an individual an advantage in any organization, it simply isn't enough in an era of rapid-change and global competition. These realities have turned the concept of job or career security into a distant memory for most people who work in virtually every sector of our dynamic economy. Having the ability to adapt to a workplace that is in a constant state of change is a necessity for those who will thrive in their careers in the years ahead.

Developing a proactive career mindset is hard work and must be sustained throughout your career. It involves a dedication to lifelong learning and personal development. It is not incompatible with providing an employer with loyal service for many years. In fact, dedicating yourself to ongoing personal development through additional training and education will often lead to enhanced opportunities for growth within your current organization. Organizations of all sizes collectively spend billions of dollars each year on employee development and education. This strategic investment benefits the organization through increased productivity and the employee through increased skills. Jump at every opportunity to enhance your skill set.

Make A Commitment To Lifelong Learning

Does your current employer offer any type of educational assistance? Many do and this is one benefit that I find employees often underutilize. The most important assets we all have are the talents and skills we bring to our jobs and careers. The best way to develop your talents and skills is through advanced education and training. Ask yourself, "Where do your skills stand right now?" If your job were eliminated today, would you have the skills to find a new job or career within a short period of time? If your answer is no, consider obtaining the appropriate training to update your skills.

Let's say your current work involves serving customers in some capacity. Your annual performance reviews have indicated that you possess terrific "people skills," but you have a fear of public speaking or you hate writing or you aren't comfortable with technology. Being deficient in any of these areas will limit your career growth. We all have weaknesses and areas where we excel. The key is to shore up our glaring weaknesses with additional training and to advance our areas of excellence through targeted development.

Once you commit to "lifelong learning" you'll provide yourself with more job or career opportunities and you'll put yourself in position to adapt to the ever-changing global economic environment. But remember this takes commitment and hard work. That's why the minority of people in the workforce today have developed the proactive career mindset.

Consider This:

Your job performance and income will be limited by your weakest skill. Increasing your competence in the weakest skill set you possess will have the most dramatic impact on your overall results than anything else you can do to advance your career.

Our key to economic survival is our ability to adapt to the rapid changes in our global economy. Developing a proactive mindset will not guarantee anyone success. It will, however, provide the best opportunity for individuals to thrive in our economy of the twenty first century. Development of a proactive career mindset will help you to achieve financial wellness in every stage of your life.

Embrace Career Change

My grandfathers and my father worked their entire careers for the same company, General Motors Corporation. A generation ago, working for the same company for an entire career was not uncommon. In fact, it was rare for people to work for multiple employers in a career when my father was in his prime working years in the 1960s and 1970s. If you are under 40 years of age and you have not worked for multiple employers, you are in the minority in this country. *The average 34 year old has worked for 9 different employers already!*[1] This rapid job changing will only accelerate as our economy transforms itself from one based on manufacturing to information based, knowledge businesses that change as fast as a click on your keyboard mouse!

Employment turnover varies by age. Average job tenure in the U.S. is about 4 years. Job tenure increases with amount of time in the workforce, with the longest tenure of 9.9 years credited to those between the ages of 55 and 64.[2] During the U.S. Department of Labor's twenty year period of job tenure analysis, virtually every age and gender category experienced a decline in average tenure with an employer. It is anticipated that this trend will accelerate based on the globalization of goods and services.

The swift pace at which we will change jobs and employers throughout our careers necessitates that we develop skills that are transferable to other industries. With the fact that most of us will have multiple employers, it will be absolutely essential to develop the financial skills to carefully choose retirement, healthcare and other employer-sponsored benefits made available to us at the worksite.

Employers will continue to shift the responsibility (and the cost) of funding retirement, healthcare and other benefits to employees. Making wise decisions about employer-sponsored benefits will impact us well beyond our working years. Our attainment of financial wellness will depend upon how we manage, fund, select and utilize the retirement, healthcare and other benefits made available by our employer.

Follow Your Passion—It's a Key Element to Financial Wellness

What makes you tick? What is it that really interests you? Can you make a living following your career passion? Think about the people you know. Aren't you amazed at how many of them really dislike their jobs or careers? I'm puzzled by the number of people who continue working at a job they truly detest, often for years! Life is simply too short to get stuck in a job or career you dislike. By developing the proactive career mindset, you'll never be stuck *for years* in a career that you truly dislike. When you develop the proactive career mindset, you are naturally inclined to pursue your passion through the necessary preparation and training to succeed.

Most of our waking hours are spent at work. That's why it's important for your overall wellness to choose a job or career that fits your interests, talents and level of training. The Gallup Organization is famous for its work in surveys and organizational development. In a landmark Gallup publication entitled: *First, Break All The Rules*, the Gallup authors identified talents as "recurring patterns of individual thoughts or behaviors that produce measurable individual outcomes."[3] Talents are extremely difficult for an individual to acquire through training. Most talents are innate, meaning we have talent in a given area or we don't. Talents are therefore part of our "genetic code." We all possess unique talents; that's why it is critical to discover your natural talents and to match them to your career.

Training can refine our individual talents and can allow individuals to excel in their careers. Gallup found that matching the talent with the job was an absolutely necessary ingredient for career success.[4] Do your talents match your current position? If so, take the time and effort to build on those talents to keep you challenged and growing. *If not, take the time to find out your true talents and do everything possible to align those talents with your job.* When your talents and your career are properly aligned, you'll put yourself in a position to succeed. Once you've aligned your talents with your job, seek to become an "expert" in an area that is critical to your organization's success. *When you develop specialized expertise in topics that are of critical necessity to your organization, your career opportunities should start to take off.* To become an expert in anything worthwhile takes a dedication to extra work and careful study of the selected area for development. There simply is no shortcut to success for most people. To become an expert in any area, you must be willing to devote considerable time and effort to developing the knowledge and experience to master a chosen subject area.

Consider Career Counseling

Often it is difficult to determine our unique talents. Career counseling professionals and organizations can be very helpful in assessing our talents. There are a variety of aptitude tests that can identify your unique talents. I'd also recommend that you supplement any testing with objective career counseling from someone experienced in helping individuals find good career matches. Be sure to check the career counselor's credentials and references before proceeding with in-depth counseling.

I took advantage of a good career counselor a few years ago and found the experience to be quite revealing about my unique career interests and talents. The time and effort I spent in this process has helped me to stay focused on my career and personal objectives. Professional career counseling has definitely had a positive impact on my overall wellness. Many career counselors also serve as ongoing career mentors, or career coaches. A good career coach can help you to achieve new goals and to help you to stay focused on career and personal development.

Update Your Resume

Do you have a current resume? I'm surprised how many people don't have their resumes updated. Why is this important? When I look back on my career thus far, the best opportunities I've had have generally come at times when I least expected it. Having an updated resume is absolutely essential. A key advantage of an updated resume is that it allows you to assess your career progress and it can also serve as an early warning sign to update skills that will be required to keep pace with the changing needs of today's workforce.

Prepare the first draft of your resume and consider having it critiqued and edited by a professional resume writer. The money you spend on this service will be well worth it for most people. A professional resume writer has the advantage of writing resumes for a living. He or she will be in tune with the style and substance needed for your resume to reflect your unique talents and experiences. Once you've established your resume, make sure that you update it at least annually to reflect any new accomplishments and to eliminate any areas that are no longer relevant in your career. Keep your resume updated to take advantage of opportunities that often appear when you'll least expect them.

Seek Career Balance

To attain financial wellness, it's essential that your career demands allow you to have a sense of balance in your personal life. Balancing career with personal needs is a daunting task. Some people can live fully balanced lives working in excess of 50 hours per week. Others will find the rigors of a 40 hour week too draining to attain the balance needed for personal and family needs. Although there is no "textbook" answer regarding the amount of time and energy one should spend on a career, it is absolutely essential that a career should not become the central focus of anyone's life. Make sure that your career allows you the balance needed to live a fulfilling life. Financial wellness cannot be obtained if your career continually overshadows the necessary balance that we all need to live a full and meaningful life. You know that your life is out of balance when your career defines who you are. If you find that this is the case, work at establishing your true "self" outside the working environment. When your career and personal priorities are in balance, you'll find a greater level of satisfaction in all facets of your life. Balance between career and personal priorities is not an "either or" proposition. It is a fine balance between two areas that need to "coexist" to enjoy the immense benefits of a rewarding career and a fulfilling personal life.

My Personal Career Revelation

Prior to my current position, most of my work involved extensive overnight travel. Although I was paid well in these positions, I realized that I was missing the opportunity to spend adequate time with my spouse and my two children. When my oldest child turned 9, I began to realize that I was missing out on a number of his school and after school activities. I was also putting a lot of pressure on my spouse during my long absences from home. I knew that I didn't want my travel to interfere with my ability to spend an appropriate amount of time with my family. So what did I do? I put together a plan to find a challenging career where I could be home most nights with my family. It took me quite a bit of time and effort and it ultimately involved a career change. Although I could be earning more money if I had stayed in my previous career, my financial discipline has allowed me to live a much more fulfilling personal life and I can now take the time to be with my children for their events and activities. The impact this has had on my life and my overall wellness is truly priceless!

Prepare for the Future

It is essential that you prepare yourself for the inevitable changes that you will experience in your career. Career changes will surely cause discomfort, but you must prepare yourself for rapid change. Develop a "proactive mindset" throughout your career. No matter how good your current employment situation is or how "secure" your job may be, your employment situation will change and you must prepare yourself to have the training and skills required in our rapidly changing global economy. Follow your passions and make sure that your work life provides you and your family with adequate balance so that you can also have a fulfilling personal life. Life is all about choices and so is your career. Never put your career on "autopilot." *And always remember that it is your responsibility to invest your time and effort in building your career skills.*

Take the time to review and complete the *Action Step Checklist* on the following page. When completed, let's move to **Step #3** in our journey to financial wellness by examining in more detail how spending decisions ranging from small, discretionary expenses to large ticket purchases shape our financial well-being…

2

ACTION STEP CHECKLIST

Step #2 Action Step Checklist

Congratulations on completing Step # 2—you are on your way to building financial wellness! When you've finished the Action Step, place a ✓ next to the Step to document your progress.

Here is your Action Step Checklist from Step #2:

- ______Examine your current job skills. Are there areas for improvement in your skills that will help you in the future? Do your current skills and level of training/education put you in a position to compete for your "next" job?

- ______Develop a proactive mindset toward your career. Commit to lifelong learning and understand that the only guarantee you have in a job is that it will change. Don't get left behind. Commit to improving your skills throughout your lifetime.

- ______Identify your interests. Does your current job match your talents and skills? If you are not sure what your true talents are or where your career path is going, consider career counseling.

- ______Is your resume updated? Even if you are not looking for employment elsewhere, an updated resume is essential in today's rapidly changing environment. If you are seeking a promotion or a different job within your current organization, a current resume will provide your new boss with a snapshot of your key accomplishments and credentials.

- ______Are your career goals and personal life in balance? If not, consider making changes so that you have a healthy balance of both in your life.

- ______Assess your personal relationships. Having solid personal relationships is a critical element in attaining long-term financial wellness. If you need help in this area, work on improved communications or consider professional counseling, if appropriate.

3

STEP 3
Always Live Beneath Your Financial Means

"The best vehicle to drive is one that's paid for."

RULE #1 FOR LIVING A FINANCIALLY BALANCED LIFE is to *always live beneath your financial means*, the title of this chapter. In the excellent book, *The Millionaire Next Door*,[1] the authors identified seven traits that millionaires in their study possess. The first, and I believe the most important trait, is that they live well below their means. I'm not advocating that everyone should measure their financial success by striving to accumulate one million dollars or more in wealth. But spending less than you can afford, especially on big ticket items such as housing and transportation, can really free up dollars you can put to work for long-term goals such as education or retirement. This mindset also serves to "trickle down" to the smaller, daily financial decisions we all make. Take a look at how much you routinely spend each day on small items such as snacks and lunches out. People who develop the mindset to live beneath their means have developed good habits in their daily spending patterns. By making common sense decisions about daily spending choices, they have the necessary resources to fund long-term savings and investments.

Buying A Home—A Pillar To Long-Term Financial Wellness

Purchasing a house is the largest single investment most people make. Buying a home has many benefits, including the use of financial leverage (you get this when you borrow money to buy a home) and tax advantages (which include tax deductibility of both mortgage interest and property taxes). And best of all, most homes will increase in value over time, giving the owner a gain on his/her investment. **Exhibit 3-1** illustrates the magnitude of household net worth differences between those who own homes and those who rent. Homeowners had a median net worth of $184,400 compared with just $4,000 for renters![2] It's no surprise, therefore, that when most people retire, the largest single investment they have is the value of their home, especially if they own it with no mortgage debt.

Remember that real estate is a long-term investment. If you are just starting your career or if you are unsettled regarding your current career, it will probably make good sense to rent a property until you have established a career. *Once you feel comfortable with both your career and where you live, buying a home you can comfortably afford can be a terrific investment and is a requisite for building long-term financial wellness.* By making interest paid on mortgage loans deductible for computing federal income taxes, the government subsidizes home ownership. Securing an affordable mortgage represents a low-cost way to build long-term equity.

Exhibit 3-1—Median Family Net Worth by Housing Status Source: Federal Reserve 2004 Triennial Survey of Consumer Finances

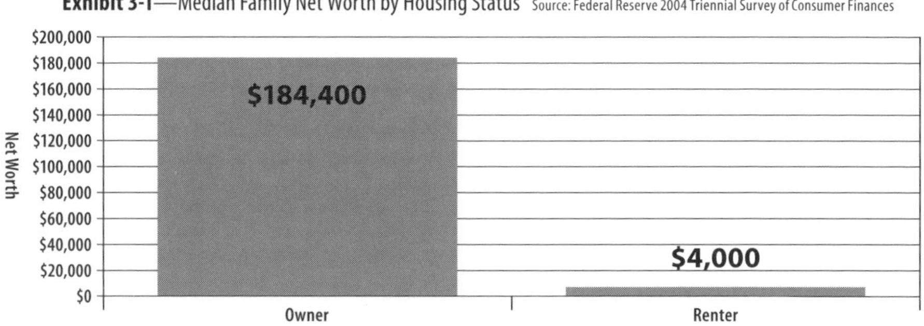

When Do You Know You're Ready?

When you are considering buying a home, commit to living in it for at least four years. *Why four years?* Closing and other costs associated with buying and selling your home will lower any gain you may experience at the time of sale. Often, it takes four years of rising home prices to offset transaction costs. The first major cost occurs when you buy your home. You will pay closing costs for the privilege of obtaining your mortgage. Depending on the type of financing you choose, closing costs could amount to several thousand dollars, especially if your loan includes "points." Paying points lowers a mortgage's interest rate by pre-paying dollars for a lower interest rate. Each point equals 1% of the loan amount. If you borrow $150,000, for example, each point will cost you $1,500! Sure, you will save money on your lower mortgage rate, but it will take years of these savings to offset the initial cost of the points. As a result, be wary of paying mortgage points unless you plan to live in the home for several years.

Another material cost is the expense of selling your home. Most homes are sold through realtors. The commission paid to realtors typically ranges from 5 to 7 percent of your final selling price. Typically, sellers pay the commissions, not buyers. When you add up the cost to buy your home and the cost to sell your home, you will need to experience price appreciation of at least 10 percent on your property to breakeven. Unless you live in a red-hot real estate market, chances are that you'll be lucky to break even, after accounting for all your buying and selling transaction expenses, in less than 4 years. If you don't see yourself living in an area for at least 4 years, I'd strongly suggest renting. Renting gives you much more flexibility should you decide to take a new job in a different city. By carefully negotiating your rental lease, you may be able to terminate your lease with a 30 day notice, giving you added flexibility. The key with renting is to find an apartment or house you can afford in a convenient location. Location is crucial whether renting or owning a home. Make sure you choose a location that has the amenities that are important to you (good schools, close to work, low crime rate, etc.).

Does Your Home Own You?

Many people get into loads of financial trouble buying houses requiring monthly payments higher than they can comfortably afford. So how much is too much? Lenders will often use a ratio that is called the "top debt ratio." This ratio takes the sum of the monthly amount needed for your mortgage, property taxes and property insurance and divides this amount by your total (gross before taxes and deductions) monthly household income. *Your top debt ratio should generally not exceed 25 to 30 percent of your gross monthly household income.* Here's an example of how to apply the "top debt ratio" to your situation:

Top Debt Ratio Illustration:

Let's assume your total household gross monthly income is $5,000. As a result, your mortgage, property taxes and property insurance for a month should not exceed $1,500. ($5,000 x .30= $1,500). The top debt ratio result can easily be calculated by this simple method. Consider an even lower ratio if your income stream is unpredictable, as is often the case with those who work in sales, where commissions can vary considerably from year to year.

Take a look at your top debt ratio to see where you stand. Beware that some realtors and mortgage brokers will suggest that you buy more home than you can comfortably afford based on the top debt ratio formula, and there are lenders who will lend you more than you can comfortably pay. Why is it so important to keep your monthly mortgage obligations under 30% of your gross monthly income? When you have more than 30% of your gross income tied up in monthly mortgage-related payments, you lose both the financial flexibility to allocate spending to other areas in your spending plan and the financial resources to cope with financial emergencies. As a result, it will be more daunting trying to reach long-term financial goals when your top debt ratio exceeds 30% of your gross monthly income.

Mortgage Length—15 or 30 Years?

Fill a room with financial and mortgage lending experts and you'll quickly get lively disagreement regarding the ideal length for a mortgage. The true answer to the appropriate length of a mortgage is "it depends." Factors influencing whether the length of the loan should be 15 or 30 years include:

- **Your age**—most people should plan to have a mortgage paid in full before retirement. So if you are over the age of 45, favor the 15 year mortgage.

- **Your mortgage payment**—a 30 year loan repayment might be the only feasible option you have to get your total debt ratio below 30%. You'll often pay about one-half of one percent more for a 30 year mortgage versus a 15 year mortgage, but the payments will be lower. Lenders require the extra interest to compensate them for the additional risk associated with longer mortgage terms—more stuff happens over 30 years than 15.

- **Your mortgage interest rate**—if you can secure a fixed mortgage rate for less than 8%, you might want to go with a 30 year instead of a 15 year fixed rate mortgage and invest the difference in long-term investments like stock mutual funds. This strategy makes sense if you have saving and investment discipline. If your long-term gains from investing exceed your mortgage rate, you'll come out ahead. The average return on large company stocks is about 10 percent per year. However, stocks can experience years of returns below 10 percent, including years of losses. Make sure that you have a timeframe of several years for stock investments. This will give you a better probability of earning a higher overall average return, which may exceed the cost of your mortgage.

- **Your goals for long-term debt**—there is absolutely nothing wrong with being debt-free at some predetermined point in time. If the thought of having debt for 30 years seems out of line with your goals or risk tolerance, choose a 15 year mortgage. It will allow you to build equity faster than a 30 year mortgage and you'll be debt free sooner.

A Look At Refinancing

Lenders are virtually everywhere you look enticing you to refinance your home. The good news with refinancing is that brutal competition among mortgage lenders has resulted in lower refinancing charges. Due to the enhanced competition for mortgage refinances, lenders will often extend favorable terms. It used to be that refinancing made sense if you could lower your mortgage rate by two percentage points or more. But, with lower closing fees, it sometimes makes sense to refinance for as little as a one percentage point reduction.

Avoid the temptation to sign on for introductory "teaser rates" that adjust in six months to a year. These rates are often tied to an "index" that is usually quite a bit higher than the rate you will be paying for the introductory period. *I believe most people should be conservative when choosing mortgage options.* As such, most people will benefit from securing a fixed rate mortgage for a term of 15 or 30 years. A good source for checking mortgage rates in your area is bankrate.com.[3]

Variable rate mortgages can make sense if you plan to live in your current home for less than seven years or if mortgage rates are at historical highs. If you choose a variable rate mortgage, know when the mortgage will adjust and which index is used for interest rate adjustments. Some will adjust annually, every three years, every five years or at some other interval. Know how long the loan amortization period is on the variable loan. Most variable loan mortgage rates will follow a 30 year amortization period. (Amortization is the amount of time it takes to retire a loan. Therefore, a monthly payment to amortize a 15 year loan will be higher than a monthly payment to amortize a 30 year loan.)

Here are a few additional points to consider when refinancing your home:

- **Get at least 3 mortgage estimates in writing**—ask each mortgage lender to make a *"Good Faith Estimate"* of all anticipated costs in writing. This will help you compare the fees each charges for mortgage services.

- **Determine how long you plan to stay in your current home**—this can have an impact on whether you take a fixed or variable rate loan. The shorter the time you plan to live in your home, the more significant the fixed fees become, because you will have fewer years to recoup mortgage expenses. Make sure you will continue to live in your house long enough to recoup them.

- **Plan how much you need to refinance**—some people seek refinancing for long-term goals such as funding a child's college education expenses or to access accumulated equity for long-term investment purposes. Know in advance how much you'll need to ensure a smooth refinance process.

- **Evaluate fixed and variable rate options for 15 and 30 year periods**—make sure you understand the options and conditions associated with each type of mortgage. If there does not seem to be a significant difference between fixed and variable rates, choose fixed for the guarantee that the rate won't change during the life of the loan.

Refinancing can make good sense when interest rates fall. Be careful not to take too much "equity" from your house in a refinance. You should make sure that you keep at least a 20 percent equity cushion when refinancing to avoid higher interest rate charges and private mortgage insurance charges.

What's Private Mortgage Insurance?

Private mortgage insurance (PMI) is charged by lenders when your home equity value is below 20% of your home's appraised market value. Lenders charge about one-half of one percent of the loan amount, or about $41.67 per month on a $100,000 loan. *Payments for PMI are not tax deductible.* PMI insurance covers the lender for the increased risk that your home may not have sufficient equity value in the event you cannot continue to make payments and you are forced by the lender into foreclosure.

Federal law requires lenders to cancel charges for PMI when the loan-to-home value ratio reaches 78 percent (PMI cancellation value). Lenders are also required to show borrowers how long it will take to reach the point of PMI cancellation in their mortgage closing documents.

If you live in an area where home values have been increasing rapidly and you think your home's market value exceeds the PMI cancellation value, contact your mortgage lender. You will probably need an independent home appraisal to satisfy the lender that your home's value exceeds the PMI cancellation value. Eliminating PMI (if applicable) could result in considerable savings.

Your home is not only an investment, it's where you live. It pays to be conservative with your home's equity and with your financing. If there is less than one percentage point between a variable and fixed mortgage rate, favor the fixed rate mortgage due to its predictability throughout the life of your loan. If you are within 15 years of retirement, be very careful when refinancing. Few people who have attained financial wellness have sizeable mortgages in their retirement years. Make it a priority to enter your retirement years debt free.

Variable Rate Loans Shift Interest Rate Risk To You

Remember that variable rate mortgages expose you to interest rate risk. You are at risk for paying a higher mortgage payment if interest rates rise. If they rise significantly, and you also face an increase in your property tax assessment (which is highly likely in most real estate markets), you get the "double-whammy" associated with a higher mortgage payment and higher property taxes. This can really put an unpleasant dent into your monthly budget. Another potential disadvantage of choosing a variable rate mortgage is that if your rate rises significantly at the time of adjustment, chances are that fixed rate mortgages will also be higher and could be harder to obtain, especially if you've had an adverse change in your overall income due to a job change or the loss of a job in your household.

Check for caps in the variable rate adjustment from one period to the next and over the lifetime of the loan. There are two caps in a variable rate mortgage. The first cap represents the most the interest rate can increase in any one year. The second cap involves the maximum amount the interest rate can increase over the life of the loan. For example, if you secure a two percent annual increase maximum, six percent lifetime adjustment "cap" variable rate loan, your mortgage cannot increase by more than 2 percentage points each year. The sum of all annual increases cannot exceed more than 6 percentage points over the life of the loan. These caps serve to limit your exposure to rising interest rates on both an annual basis and over the life of your mortgage.

Buyer Beware!

Beware of the option adjustable rate mortgage! This is a very seductive type of variable rate mortgage that seems almost too good to be true at the beginning of the loan. (We all should know that when something sounds too good to be true, it almost always is!) These loans are complicated and have become popular in over-heated real estate markets, because they give home buyers the ability to get into a home with below-market interest rates. Some even allow negative amortization of unpaid interest by adding unpaid interest to the principal balance. This is not a prudent way to purchase a home or build long-term home equity.

My advice for these types of mortgages is to stay away! If you can't afford a home with a conventional fixed rate or a conventional adjustable rate, find a lower priced home you can afford. If you are in an option adjustable rate mortgage, read the contract you signed and know your mortgage options. Ignorance of the financing rules will probably hurt you financially. Consider seeking other mortgage financing, if feasible.

Know Thyself

Take stock of your personal situation, and estimate the monthly payment you can afford. When you carefully consider your circumstances, choose a mortgage amortization period and a fixed or variable rate option that works best for you. *If in doubt about which option is best for you, consider the fixed rate 30 year mortgage.* You'll have a lower required monthly payment that will stay the same over the life of your mortgage, and you'll free up money for other uses. If you find that you have excess cash or that your income has grown substantially, you can always pay down your mortgage. Make sure your mortgage allows you to pre-pay without penalty. Most mortgages allow prepayment. Adding small sums to your mortgage principal, especially in the early years of your mortgage, can reduce the duration of your loan considerably. For example, if your mortgage payment is $570 per month, consider rounding it up to $600. You'll pay off your mortgage sooner, and save tons of interest over the life of your loan. Take the time to "run the numbers" with your mortgage lender and choose the mortgage that works best for your situation.

Vehicle Purchases And Leases—Handle With Care

One of the biggest mistakes I see people make continually involves the purchase or lease of vehicles. Purchases or leases involving vehicles represent the second largest expenditure by most people. *First, unlike buying a home, understand that a vehicle is not an investment that has any reasonable likelihood of increasing in value.* Sure, some vehicles are of a higher quality, and they don't lose their value as quickly as others, but make no mistake that the vehicle you purchase today will likely be worth considerably less in the future. Vehicles are costly to purchase or lease, they need routine maintenance, repairs, insurance and some models are gas guzzlers. All of this adds up to a real "money pit" for your limited hard earned dollars. The key decision to make when purchasing or leasing a vehicle is to seek dependable transportation at the right price.

A Key Discovery

I was intrigued to learn from *The Millionaire Next Door* research that 37 percent of millionaires interviewed for a vehicle purchase survey reported purchasing used vehicles, and that the average millionaire spent under $25,000 for his/her most recent new automobile purchase. The survey dates back to the mid 1990s, but even so, $25,000 bought a relatively modest vehicle for a millionaire. If you've looked at the sticker price for new vehicles in the past couple of years, you'll quickly discover that $25,000 doesn't come close to buying a "luxury" vehicle today. In fact, with basic optional equipment, it would be a challenge for most people to purchase a new vehicle for under $25,000. So what's the lesson here? Be smart like a millionaire—keep your vehicle spending in line with your overall spending plan, and do adequate homework before making a decision about purchasing or leasing a vehicle. Seek reliability, safety and price over status and the latest optional features that can tack thousands on to the price of your vehicle. Also remember, you aren't what you drive!

Here's a list of 7 key factors to consider when purchasing or leasing a vehicle.

1. **If you decide to purchase a new vehicle, seek incentives offered by the manufacturer.** Never pay the sticker price. There are a number of websites that can help you to determine a fair price for a new or used vehicle. One of my favorites is Edmunds.com.[4]

2. **Lease with caution.** Leasing is seductive because leases can be structured in a variety of ways to make leasing look inexpensive. For example, most leases have a total mileage limit. Often the standard limit is about 12,000 miles per year. Exceed the limit and you have some hefty extra charges for the extra mileage at the end of your lease. Additional mileage charges often range from 15 to 30 cents per extra mile driven, saddling you with an unpleasant final payment to conclude your lease obligation. To make matters worse, at the end of your lease, you don't have a vehicle. You then have to decide to either purchase the leased vehicle or move on to another vehicle and the entire cycle of monthly payments starts all over again! Now you know why many financial planners refer to leases as "fleeces"—unless you are careful, you can be fleeced by a lease!

If you decide to lease, never pay cash up front for the privilege of leasing. That's simply throwing your money away and gives the impression that the lease is less costly than it is. It appears less costly because the down payment reduces the monthly lease payment amount. Ask the dealer to quote the lease without any lease down payment. You'll get a true picture of the monthly cash outflow needed for the lease, and you'll be able to compare the leasing payment to the cost of vehicle purchase.

A significant factor in the overall cost of a lease is the vehicle's "residual value" at the end of the lease.[5] Find out this number, and ask the dealer which vehicles offer the highest residual value at the conclusion of the lease. This may encourage you to look at a different model, but it could save you quite a bit in monthly lease payments due to the higher ending residual value. Finally, if you don't understand the terms and financial conditions of the lease, chances are you are not getting a good deal. With leases, remember to proceed with extreme caution!

3. **Consider** *(and this is my recommended strategy for most people)* **buying a 2-3 year old vehicle with under 30,000 miles.** Why? You can get virtually any make and model for no more than half of the vehicle's price when it was purchased new. You also get the advantage of buying the vehicle while it is still under the manufacturer's warranty in case something should go wrong after your purchase. (Most manufacturers offer at least a 3 year 36,000 mile transferable warranty on new vehicles.) Also consider having a "background check" performed on the vehicle you are considering. I recommend using CARFAX, carfax.com. For about $25 you can find out invaluable information about the history of most vehicles. Your report will highlight important facts

including how many owners the vehicle has had, major accidents, etc. If the vehicle you are considering has had a history of accidents, multiple owners, or anything that looks suspect, you should probably move on to another vehicle.

4. **Say no to most expensive end of sale items like extended warranties and special interior or exterior sealants designed to keep your vehicle running and looking better longer.** Most extended warranties are simply too expensive for what you receive in return. They are loaded with coverage exclusions, front end deductibles, and a host of other items, making your hefty cash outlay a bad deal for you and a good one for the dealer and the company backing the warranty. Skip the interior and exterior sealants, as they are usually a poor value for the amount you'll be asked to pay.

5. **Seek practicality over style.** Assess your driving situation, need for space for transporting others, such as children, and investigate the vehicle's fuel economy and cost to insure. Don't overlook insurance costs. Some models are much more expensive to insure than others due to higher repair costs, safety issues, and frequency of theft. A call to your insurance agent prior to purchase can save you from making an expensive insurance mistake. Find out from your insurance agent which models are the lowest to insure and why.

6. **Keep financing on new vehicles to no more than 48 months.** For used vehicles, seek a loan term of no longer than 36 months. Here's why. Since most vehicles lose their value quickly, longer financing terms put you in danger of owing more on your vehicle than its worth, an unpleasant situation known as being upside down. Don't put yourself into this situation.

7. **Once your vehicle is paid in full, drive it as long as possible.** That's where you will really start to see the benefits of extra cash that can be used for other purposes. There's an old saying about becoming wealthy: *When it's time to get rid of your car, make it last one more year.* Sure, you will pay more in repairs and maintenance, but the lack of a monthly payment usually can pay for a considerable amount of repairs. Since your car will be worth less when it is older, your insurance rates should be much lower than rates for a more expensive model. *To make this strategy work for you, make sure your vehicle receives scheduled maintenance.* A well maintained vehicle lasts much longer and is more reliable. Potential problems are often diagnosed before a costly and inconvenient breakdown occurs. Your owner's manual will have a listing of scheduled maintenance intervals for your vehicle. Follow this schedule to get the maximum life and performance from your vehicle.

Items #3 and #7 above represent my best advice regarding your decision to purchase a vehicle. Notice that I left out leasing as the best value for most people. Once the lease is over, that's it. You start the cycle of spending all over again. By purchasing a late model vehicle and holding it for as long as possible, you will go a long way in minimizing overall vehicle expenses.

Look At The Small Expenses—These Can Break A Budget

Small expenses often fall under an area that I call "impulse spending." In this area, you'll want to look at how you spend money in discretionary areas such as dining out, recreation and clothing expenses. These are the big "three" for most people. With our fast-paced, time-starved schedules, dining out has become a way of life for many of us. Look at where you're spending your money in this area and make adjustments to your spending.

Consider This:

Try packing lunches more frequently. I do this quite often. Not only do I eat better, but I save a bundle in the cost of expensive lunches.

Recreation is another area where spending can get out of hand. Look at your spending habits for the activities you enjoy. You'll probably find ways to save considerably in this area. For clothing, do you really need the latest fashion designs or can you get by with what you have? You may be able to enjoy large savings by buying your clothes out of season when huge discounts apply.

How we spend our income often has more to do with what we value as important (a want) more than our true needs. One technique that I often use to keep my personal spending in check is to challenge myself when I'm faced with spending decisions. I ask myself: "Will this purchase improve my life? Why do I want this item? Are there alternatives? What if I wait to purchase when the item goes on sale?" I've developed a mindset that challenges my desire to accumulate material items. It's not to say that I don't purchase items that I don't truly need, but knowing the difference between a true need and a discretionary purchase has saved me literally thousands of dollars over the past 25 years.

Here's a list of common discretionary purchases that can have a real impact on your ability to reach long-term financial goals. Try to keep these expenses in check to free up dollars to follow Rule #1 of this chapter (living beneath your means):

- **Dining out**—cut out one lunch from a restaurant each week and save $40 per month. Do the same with one dinner out and free up $30-$60 per month. Getting in the habit of packing a lunch can save you big bucks over the course of a year, and likely is healthier.

- **Entertainment**—if you like movies, consider a membership in a DVD movie club instead of spending top-dollar to go to the theatre to see the latest movie release. If you routinely go out on the town twice a week, consider moving it back to one night per week and use the evening you've freed up to pursue a hobby or special interest from home such as reading. Get a library card from your local public library. This is truly one of the best values going today. Most libraries allow you to check out books and movies at low or no cost. Plus you can often find some of your favorite magazines in the magazine section. Don't overlook this incredible value.

- **Clothing**—think "on sale" for just about everything you or your family members wear. With retailers offering sales virtually every day on selected items, find out when items you want will go on sale or search the Internet for sale items. Also, if you are thinking of purchasing a big-ticket item such as a suit or expensive pair of shoes, ask the retailer for a discount on the purchase. I've done this often and the majority of the time, I either get a discount or get something else (that I need) such as free alterations. It doesn't hurt to ask for a discount—don't be shy to ask!

- **Telephone and Internet service**—big savings are often "just a phone call or click away!" With increasing competition for all types of communication services (broadband, DSL, Voice over Internet Protocol, etc.), you'll probably find monthly savings available if you take the time to look at your options. If you come to the conclusion that changing is too big a hassle, use the advertised prices from your current carrier's competitors to lower your price. I've done this many times to lower my broadband bill. I just combined my broadband Internet service with my telephone service. This switch gives me unlimited calls within the U.S. and Canada for a low monthly fixed rate. The result of combining all services with my Internet broadband provider is a savings of about $60 per month.

- **Big-ticket items**—Think sale price on virtually every purchase that falls under this category. Items such as appliances, furniture, carpeting and vacations can usually be found on sale. In fact, I have a rule to never buy furniture unless it is on sale. I research pricing on the Internet and make my move once I know that I have struck a great deal. The same is true with vacations. There are deals galore, but it takes planning and a little flexibility to realize big-time savings!

- **Newspapers and magazine subscriptions**—consider going online for your news information. Most major newspapers have an online service that is often free. You can also find websites for major magazines that are also free. By cutting back on your ongoing subscriptions and using online or library sources, you'll save a few more dollars that will allow you to comfortably "live beneath your means" to free up money for other purposes.

Make Solid Choices

We all live on a limited amount of income. Some people make considerably more than others. But it's what we manage to keep and invest from our hard work that truly puts us on a path to financial wellness. By making good spending decisions and committing to live beneath your means, you'll position yourself to reach your financial goals. You'll also noticeably reduce stress related to your finances when you've made the decision to live beneath your means. This will have an impact on every facet of your life and will serve as a powerful catalyst for achieving long-term financial wellness.

Consider This:

In my experience, what separates financially healthy people from everyone else is their ability to control their spending, not their ability to earn money.

Take the time to review and complete the *Action Step Checklist* on the following page. Upon completion of the *Checklist*, let's now move to Step #4 and look at how you can set yourself free from unnecessary debt...

3
ACTION STEP CHECKLIST

Step #3 Action Step Checklist

Congratulations on completing Step #3. Listed are some key Action Steps to consider from this chapter. When you've finished the Action Step, place a ✓ next to the Step to document your progress.

Here is your Action Step Checklist from Step #3:

- ______Make home ownership a goal if you plan to live in an area for at least 4 years. Home ownership is one of the best ways to build financial wellness. Homeowners enjoy a significant net worth advantage over non-homeowners.

- ______If you own a home or are thinking of buying a home in the future, try to keep your "top debt" ratio under 30% of your gross monthly income. This amount should cover your mortgage payment, property taxes and home insurance. By keeping your top debt ratio below 30% of your gross income, you'll have budget room for other expense and investment priorities. Calculate your recommended maximum top debt ratio by multiplying your total monthly gross income (before taxes and deductions) by 30%.

- ______Select the right mortgage length for your financial goals. If in doubt, a 30 year mortgage often makes the most sense due to a lower payment (compared with a 15 year mortgage) and the ability to make extra payments in the future without penalty.

- ______Choose a fixed rate mortgage if the fixed and variable rates are within a point or two of each other. Remember, a fixed rate does not change for the life of your mortgage. Variable rate mortgages adjust periodically, and the rate you may pay in the future can be significantly higher than the "locked-in" fixed rate. Stay away from complicated adjustable rate mortgages that allow you to pay interest only or to skip payments. These mortgages are especially good at producing grief when interest rates rise and home values stagnate or fall.

- ______The best value when purchasing a vehicle is usually offered on models that are two or three years old with low miles. Once you own a vehicle, the key to getting the best value is to keep your vehicle well-maintained and to drive it for several years. If you decide to purchase new, commit to keeping the vehicle for several years. If you lease, keep the terms of your lease under the manufacturer's original warranty and avoid making a down payment on any lease.

- ______Keep an eye on the "small expenses." These can really drill a hole in your monthly budget. Consider dining out less frequently and commit to buying clothing and large ticket items on sale.

4

STEP 4
Mastering Debt

"If you want a "safe" rate of return on your money, look no further than your personal debts."

Do You Carry Monthly Credit Card Balances?

In April 2009, the average interest rate charged for a standard variable rate credit card was 14.17 percent. Many credit cards charge much higher interest rates, some in excess of 20 percent. There are no safe investments that will return anywhere close to the rate of interest charged on most credit cards. Take a look at your credit card balances. If you routinely pay your credit charges in full each month, congratulations! However, many people just pay the minimum required amount each month, incurring interest charges amounting to thousands of dollars over the term of the credit card loan.

One of the first steps to securing long-term financial wellness is getting out, and staying out, of credit card debt. Take a good look at your current use of credit cards. The first step to take if you have credit card balances is to identify the card that charges the highest interest rate and apply extra dollars to that card first. Keep in mind if you have more than one credit card with a balance, the card to pay first might **not** be the one with the highest balance. *When it comes to choosing the credit card on which to pay extra, always work to pay off the card that carries the highest interest rate charge and then move to pay off the card with the next highest interest rate.*

The Minimum Payment Credit Card Trap

Credit card companies know that many people will pay the minimum monthly charge, month after month, year after year. This is one of the ways people get into trouble with credit card debt. Paying just the minimum amount gives a false sense of security that the debt is "manageable." Guess what usually happens? New cards are secured, and over the course of time, the number and size of minimum payments becomes financially (and emotionally) overwhelming.

Example of the Minimum Payment Trap:

Assume a starting balance of $5,000, an interest rate of 18% and a minimum payment of 2.5 percent of the principal balance each month. Assuming that no new purchases are made (a very conservative assumption!), it will take 313 months or 26 years to pay the credit card debt in full! Additionally, the interest paid during the 313 months is a whopping $7,115! No wonder we receive so many credit card offers!

There are a number of credit payment calculators available for your use on the Internet. One calculator I especially like can be found on Bankrate.com's website. This calculator allows you to enter your balance, interest rate and minimum payment amount. It then provides a detailed, month-by-month schedule of principal and interest payments. The calculator will also give you the opportunity to add additional payment amounts so that you can find out how long it will take to pay the balance in full. If you are carrying a balance, check out this website and use the credit card calculator—it can serve as a handy resource as you work to pay off your credit card debt.

Consumer Debt Is Growing At Warp Speed

Consumer debt now exceeds two trillion dollars! What's the significance of two trillion dollars in consumer debt? It's the growth of this debt. In December 1994, consumer debt had just crossed the one trillion dollar mark. In a little over ten years, consumer debt had doubled! These numbers don't include mortgage debt. *A key component to attaining financial wellness is to control and eventually eliminate consumer debt.* Consider these facts:

- The average balance on a credit card is $7,000, offering an average interest rate of 18.9 percent.[2]

- Americans are now carrying $683 billion in revolving credit card debt. That's not the amount we charge every month; it's the outstanding unpaid balances on which people pay interest.[3]

- 47% of the people who paid less than the full amount on their credit card bills in a recent month made only the minimum payment due. In fact, only 13% of Americans with an outstanding balance could afford to pay more than half the balance.[4]

- More than 10% of households have monthly debts greater than their monthly incomes.[5]

- Only 25% of low-income households have credit card debt. *But 48% of zero-net-worth households do, and they owe nearly twice the average amount.*[6]

Rates Vary Considerably

If you must carry a balance, be sure to shop around for a card that carries the lowest interest charge. Why do rates for debt vary so much? A major factor involves the risk the lender is willing to take to extend you credit. When debt is secured by an asset such as a home or an automobile, lenders will usually charge much less for this form of "secured debt." A good example of unsecured debt involves credit card purchases. If you fail to pay your credit card debt, the lender will have a much more difficult time collecting the debt owed, because the debt is not secured by a specific asset like an automobile or a home. In banking terms the *default risk* associated with credit card debt is higher and therefore the interest rate charged reflects the additional risk the lender takes in extending unsecured credit.

How's Your Credit?

Do you have good credit? You may or may not know the answer to this question. Lenders have a scoring system for determining your credit status. It's called your credit score. A particular person may have as many as 30 different credit scores depending on the credit rating bureau and on the type of bank credit used. One of the most common credit scores is the FICO score. This acronym stands for Fair Isaac & Company. This company was founded in 1956 by engineer Bill Fair and Mathematician Earl Isaac. The FICO mathematical model uses a variety of inputs related to your credit and personal history to arrive at a final score. Lenders use the FICO model when you apply for credit, especially when seeking a home mortgage.

Key inputs that affect your FICO score include:

- Late payments

- The amount of time credit has been established

- The amount of credit used versus the amount of credit available (measured by the ratio of credit card debt to total credit available)

- Length of time at present residence
- Employment history
- Negative credit information such as bankruptcies, charge-offs, collections, etc.

The higher your FICO score, the better. Scores range from 300 to 850. Any score below 620 will put you at increased risk for being denied credit. Generally a score above 620 is the minimum score needed for a mortgage loan financed by mortgage lenders Fannie Mae or Freddie Mac. If your score falls below 620 and you can find credit, it will probably be in the "sub-prime" market, where rates charged are often significantly higher than rates charged to people who have a score of 620 or higher.

There are three credit bureaus that assign a FICO score and your score may vary from bureau to bureau. Lenders will often use the middle score if there is a difference among the credit bureau FICO scores. The three bureaus that collect your FICO data are Experian, Trans Union and Equifax. You can improve your FICO score over a period of time. If your score is low, it will take time for your changes in debt payment patterns to reflect positively in your score. Here are some tips that will increase your score:

- **Pay your bills on time.** Late payments and collections can have a serious impact on your score.
- **Do not apply for credit frequently.** Having a large number of inquiries on your credit report can worsen your score.
- **Reduce your credit card balances.** If you are "maxed" out on your credit cards, your credit score will be lower.
- **If you have limited credit, obtain additional credit.** Not having sufficient credit can negatively impact your score.

How To Monitor Your Credit For Free

With credit scams running rampant and identity theft affecting millions of consumers worldwide, it's more important than ever to know what's in your credit file and to act quickly if you notice inaccurate or false information.

The Fair Credit Reporting Act requires each of the 3 major consumer credit reporting companies to provide you a free copy of your credit report (one report from each agency every 12 months) upon request. So how do you go about requesting a free credit report? There are 3 ways to do this:

1. By going online to **www.annualcreditreport.com**;

2. By phone: **1-877-322-8228**;

3. By mail: Mail a completed **Annual Credit Report Request Form** (found by going online to ftc.gov/credit) to Annual Credit Report Request Service, P.O. Box 105281, Atlanta, GA 30348-5281.

If you have online access, it's easy to order your report online. In a matter of minutes, you'll have your credit report available for your review. Since all three credit reporting services are required to send you one free credit report every 12 months, it might make sense to order one report every 4th month, each time from just one of the three services. By doing this, you'll be able to monitor your credit status throughout the year—by getting an updated credit report three times a year. However, you may order from one, two or all three credit reporting services at the same time. Also note that, while you can get a copy of your credit report, you cannot get a free copy of your credit score.

You'll also have the opportunity to order additional reports for additional fees from the credit reporting services. Unless you have or suspect a credit reporting problem, it probably makes sense for most people to stick with the free reports. The free reports will provide ample information about your credit, and will give you the necessary information to know that your credit files are accurate. *Make sure that you periodically request free credit reports so that you can identify any items that are questionable or inaccurate.*

Debt & The Power Of Financial Leverage—Caution: Use In Moderation!

When properly used, debt can provide us with a very powerful force: *financial leverage*—the ability to multiply your returns. For most people, their homes are their largest personal investment. Most people get into the housing market with a small down payment, often less than 20% of the purchase price of the property. The balance is financed by a mortgage. Repayment of the mortgage will usually range from 15 to 30 years. This common transaction produces financial leverage for homeowners.

Let's look at an example assuming the purchase of a $150,000 starter home. If the homeowner puts 20% down on the purchase (that's $30,000), the balance of $120,000 is financed. The homeowner has secured an asset with a value of at least $150,000 on the date of purchase. If the homeowner did a good job of selecting the right property, the property will appreciate over time. The good news for the homeowner is that the property appreciation is based on the total value of the property—$150,000—but the home buyer invested only $30,000. To illustrate how financial leverage works, consider the following:

Consider This:

Let's say the property in the above paragraph appreciates in value 6% in the first year. The house will increase from $150,000 to $159,000. Remember that the homeowner put in only $30,000 for the down payment. The homeowner's actual return is the $9,000 gain divided by the $30,000 down payment. This result is a return (which the property owner has not realized) of 30% on the amount invested! This is how most homeowners build wealth through the use of financial leverage and the appreciation of property over time.

Keep in mind that it will often take a few years of consistent price appreciation for homeowners to actually make money by the time they sell. The key reason involves transaction costs. It costs money to secure the mortgage, and most people must—and generally should—list their homes with realtors. *That's why most people should* plan to live in their new houses at least four years. Any less than 4 years can result in a loss to the homeowner—and that's when renting often makes the most sense.

The secret to this form of "good debt" is to use it carefully and to use it almost exclusively to purchase tangible or intangible assets that will grow in value over time. Here's a definition of good debt:

Good Debt Definition

"Good" debt is used primarily to purchase tangible assets (usually real estate) that *increase* in value over time. Good debt can also be used to fund intangible assets such as advanced education or training, which often results in increased earning power and enhanced employment opportunities. Good debt provides financial leverage to increase the earning potential of **tangible** and **intangible** assets.

Debt that produces financial leverage must be used carefully. Like most things in life, too much of a good thing often results in unintended consequences. The key to using this form of debt is to make sure that your income can support the debt payment terms.

When you use good debt wisely, you can enhance the quality of your life and increase your financial net worth prudently through the use of financial leverage. *When using debt, try to devote most debt to the purchase of assets that increase in value over time.* For most of us, this involves the purchase of real estate (housing). Real estate is a natural hedge against inflation because property values generally keep pace with inflation, and the interest paid to finance real estate purchases is almost always tax deductible.

Using Debt For College or Specialized Vocational Training

Debt that produces financial leverage is used primarily for mortgages but also applies to debt that is used to finance your own education or a family member's education. *Our ability to generate an income is by far our greatest financial asset.* The value of an education is an *intangible asset* that tends to pay dividends in the form of higher income potential over the course of a lifetime. **Exhibit 4-1** shows average annual earnings by education level. This chart illustrates the direct relationship that exists between higher education levels and higher earning potential.

Exhibit 4-1—Average Annual Earnings By Education Level Source: U.S. Census Bureau

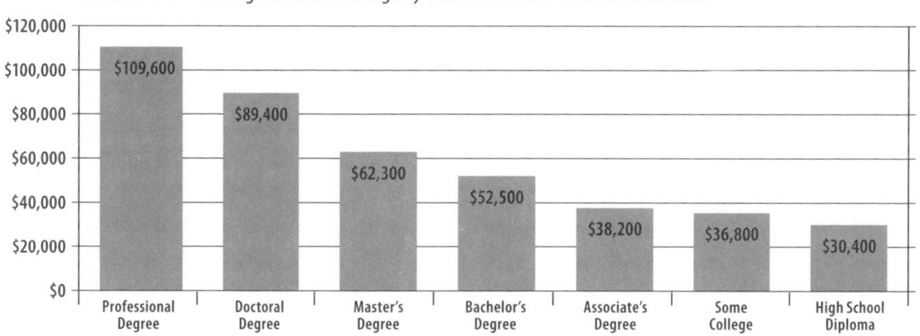

Be careful not to take on too much debt to finance your child's college education, especially if it results in under-funding your retirement savings. Remember that recent college graduates have an entire career to pay off accumulated college debts. Your retirement financial well-being needs to be your highest priority. By careful planning and saving during your child's early years, the need for debt financing for college expenses during college years will be minimized, resulting in a manageable debt load for you and your children.

Master Debt For Financial Wellness

The problem with too much debt is that it limits your long-term choices in life. It also adds considerably to individual and family stress. Debt levels often grow disproportionately as income rises. Many people get into the cycle of always stretching beyond what they can afford, regardless of income. This also applies to many six-figure income earners who overspend on housing, transportation, vacations, and a host of other areas that are controllable.

Mastering debt takes ongoing discipline. Marketers are virtually everywhere you look vying for your limited income. When you stop and think about it, we receive countless marketing messages each day from broadcast media, print media and the Internet. It's no wonder so many people have problems with too much debt: *Our options for spending money are endless, but our incomes are limited.* Here are five surefire ways to reign in debt:

1. **Freeze credit card spending.** If spending is out of control, use only cash to make purchases. It's a fact that we spend less when we use cash versus a piece of plastic. For those who like to impulse spend, consider putting your credit cards in a freezer bag filled with water and put the big freeze on them! If you need to use your card for a purchase, you'll need to wait until the water has thawed. This should put a real "chill" on urges to spend on impulse.

2. **Pay debt strategically.** Pay the highest interest rate debt first. It's the best way to get a great return on your hard-earned dollars.

3. **Assess your current lifestyle.** Go after the big-ticket items first. Transportation is usually the first place to look, because it's often easy to make changes in this big expense category. Look at your driving and how you're driving. Vehicles are big money pits. There is simply no such thing as an "investment in an automobile." Find transportation that is functional and safe to operate. Look for economy in fuel consumption and in insurability. A major change in this category can really free up funds to be used in paying off debt. Also examine your housing situation. Are there good, money saving alternatives to the apartment you're leasing or the current home you own? Transportation and housing adjustments can really turn around a budget and free up considerable dollars for debt reduction. Finally, take a look at how much you are spending on entertainment (yes, eating at a restaurant is entertainment) and vacations. Cutting back only a little can add up to hundreds of dollars in a year.

4. **Moonlight.** Yes, consider a second job until you have your debts in check. The extra income from a second job can be completely applied to debt reduction.

5. **Consolidate debt.** Take a look at all the places where you owe debt. You'll find that creditors will charge a range of interest rates. If you own a home, you may be able to consolidate debt through a home equity loan. If you're really far into debt, you may wish to seek the services of a debt counseling agency. But beware of these agencies. There are scores of agencies that really aren't worth their fees and often put their financial interests before yours. But there are many that do put your interests first. Take the time to interview any debt consolidation agency, and find out their plan for helping you with debt reduction.

Generally, look for a debt consolidation agency that has a non-profit mission. Some for-profit debt counseling firms do a great job, and some non-profits are outright scams, so make sure you understand how any debt counseling firm receives operating revenues to sustain its operations.

Many of the non-profit debt counseling firms receive substantial funding from credit issuers. There is nothing wrong with this, and it shouldn't affect the objectivity of the credit agency. Credit issuers realize that it is in their best interest to help those in credit trouble through professional guidance, giving them the best opportunity for future debt repayment. *To find a reputable consumer credit counseling agency in your area, go to the Internet and type in "Consumer credit counseling."* You'll find a host of agencies that can assist you. It will generally make the most sense to find an agency that is close to where you live so that you can develop a close working relationship with your credit counselor. Make sure you take the time to carefully interview credit counselors to ensure a good fit with your objectives.

Gaining Control Over Debt

How do you know when you are starting to master debt control? It's simple. When you no longer carry a credit card balance from month to month, you are on your way to mastering debt. By developing the discipline to pay all credit card balances each month, it's much easier to pay off your other forms of credit.

Interest rates either work for you or against you. Interest expenses accumulate 24 hours a day, seven days a week. These charges can be relentless over time. The same laws of interest compounding can work for you when you master debt and begin saving and investing for the future. By eliminating non-mortgage debt from your budget, you'll position yourself to save and invest in your future.

Once all forms of non-mortgage debt are eliminated, you can start a systematic program of investing to build financial wellness. Over a period of years, compound interest can make modest sums of money grow incredibly. When you master debt, you put yourself in a position to make your money grow for you through the power of compound interest. By "sowing the seeds" of saving and investing versus debt and spending, you set yourself up for a more secure financial future.

Take the time to review and complete the *Action Step Checklist* on the following page. Upon completion of the *Checklist*, let's move to the best place for most of us to save and invest for our financial futures—**Step #5**, employer-sponsored benefit plans…

4

ACTION STEP CHECKLIST

Step #4 Action Step Checklist

Congratulations on completing Step #4. Listed are some key Action Steps to consider from this chapter. When you've finished the Action Step, place a ✓ next to the Step to document your progress.

Here is your Action Step Checklist from Step #4:

- ______ Add up your current credit card debt. If you are carrying a balance, commit to paying off the balance with the highest interest rate first. Also, minimize or stop using credit cards unless it is an absolute emergency. Getting credit card debt to zero is a key factor in attaining long-term financial wellness.

- ______ Find out your credit history (and check for errors!) by requesting a free credit report every four months from one of the three major credit reporting agencies. Follow up on any inaccuracies or on any report item that you do not understand. Receiving ongoing free credit reports is a good way to protect yourself from identity theft.

- ______ Good debt is used to purchase tangible and intangible assets that increase in value over time. This serves to produce financial leverage if used properly. The two most common areas where "good debt" is used include home mortgages and financing advanced education or training. Be careful in the use of this form of debt because too much debt can lead to financial problems.

- ______ An investment in college or advanced skills development usually has a big payoff. Look at your current skills and make sure that you optimize your earning power through proper education and training. Find out if your employer offers training or educational opportunities to improve your skills.

- ______ Make mastery of debt a major objective in your long-term planning. Remember that too much debt limits your long-term options for savings and investment.

STEP 5
Understand And Fully Utilize Employer-Sponsored Benefits

"One of the best ways to attain financial wellness is through participation in your employer's retirement savings plan."

This is Your Wake Up Call!

Lifelong financial wellness is your responsibility. Like it or not, employers are shifting the responsibility for a secure retirement to you. For most of us the days of working for one employer for an entire career and retiring with a generous pension that pays for most retirement expenses, along with 100 percent employer-funded healthcare benefits will never occur. Although these generous benefits were the norm a generation ago for many American workers, they might seem far-fetched to you now. The new "era" most of us find at the workplace involves considerable choice in how we fund and participate in employer-sponsored benefit plans.

Why the shift? *The main reasons are cost and competitive pressures.* Benefit costs are skyrocketing, especially costs associated with pension and health insurance benefits. Brutal global competition in most industries has resulted in ever-tightening operating margins and the inability of businesses of all sizes to raise prices to cover the spiraling cost of employee benefits. The result is a rapidly changing employee benefits package that requires more employee decision making and more employee financial responsibility, especially for the payment of health insurance benefits and retirement planning.

Defined Benefit Pension Plans

If your employer covers you under a defined benefit pension plan, count your blessings! This is truly a wonderful benefit, because you are not required to contribute. Once you meet the plan's vesting requirements (which usually is measured by years of service), the pension belongs to you for use in funding your retirement expenses. Defined benefit plans are so named because a retiring worker's monthly pension—the benefit—is defined by a formula usually based on the retiring worker's years of service and recent earnings.

The defined benefit pension plan is rapidly being replaced by defined contribution 401(k)-type plans primarily due to the high cost of funding and administering defined benefit plans. This funding cost can represent a huge annual expense for employers and a source of ongoing liability for the payment of future, promised benefits.

If you are covered under a defined benefit plan, understand that the plan can be amended or future benefits "frozen" at any time. IBM and DuPont recently made massive changes to their defined benefit pension plans that will reduce future benefits for active employees. That's why it's vitally important to make contributions to defined contribution 401(k)-type plans, if offered by your employer.

In this chapter we will look at the steps you can take to maximize the benefits your employer offers. Employer-sponsored benefit plans have changed significantly over the past decade and will continue to evolve to meet corporate cost pressures and the ever-changing needs of employees and their family members. It is absolutely essential for your overall financial wellness that you use employer-sponsored benefit plans to their fullest, taking advantage of tax-deferred savings through 401(k)-type savings plans and selecting appropriate benefit plans (health, flexible spending, life insurance, etc.) to protect and enhance your overall financial well-being.

Don't Bet On Social Security For A Solid Retirement

If you are under the age of 45 and think that Social Security might provide a sustainable safety net for retirement, **think again**. The Social Security and Medicare (health insurance for the elderly) systems are headed for financial collapse unless radical changes are made to both programs. Just look at what David M. Walker, Chief of the General Accounting Office, had to say about the future of Social Security and Medicare in an interview in 2004:

> **"The public has no idea how big the problem is. The 43 trillion dollars in unfunded Social Security, Medicare and other retirement benefits will drive the federal government into insolvency by 2040 unless Congress moves quickly."**

In a testimony before the U.S. Senate Budget Committee on January 18, 2007, Federal Reserve Chairman Ben Bernanke also sounded a warning about the fiscal health of Social Security and Medicare. Mr. Bernanke stated:

"If early and meaningful action is not taken in reforming Social Security and Medicare, then the U.S. economy could be seriously weakened with future generations bearing much of the cost."

It is "politically incorrect" for any politician to mention changes to Social Security or Medicare that involve raising payroll taxes, cutting benefits or both. Understand that until Congress has the will to address this enormous problem, benefits will keep getting paid and projected deficits for these entitlement programs will continue to grow at an alarming rate. *The bottom line for all of this:* When changes to Social Security come in the future, they will probably result in lower benefits and higher payroll taxes. That's why it's more important than ever to build your retirement savings through your employer's retirement savings program.

According to the *National Center for Policy Analysis' Social Security and Medicare Report of 2005*, both entitlement programs combined will experience the following outcomes (based on intermediate projections):

- **By 2030,** about the midpoint of the baby boomer retirement years, the two programs will need more than half of all federal income taxes to fill the gap between payroll tax revenues and promised benefits.

- **By 2050,** Social Security and Medicare will require three in four income tax dollars collected, in addition to payroll taxes.

- **By 2070,** almost all federal income tax revenues will be needed to provide full promised Social Security and Medicare benefits.

These estimates are based on the *intermediate* projections, so the reality could be worse if no changes are made to the current benefits paid by both programs.[1] The report by the National Center for Policy Analysis and similar research from scores of respected experts concludes that massive changes will be needed to both Social Security and Medicare in the not-so-distant future to keep the programs afloat. This likely translates into much lower benefits for those under the age of 45. This probable scenario of lower Social Security benefits and significantly higher Medicare costs translates into more retirement costs being shifted to you during your retirement years.

Are You Taking Full Advantage Of Your Company's Benefit Plans?

If you are taking full advantage of your company's benefits programs, you are in the minority of employees. Many, if not most, employees don't understand the benefits offered by their employers. The result is inappropriate utilization of benefit options and a lost opportunity to use employer benefit plans as a primary vehicle for systematically building financial wellness. Some common employer-sponsored benefits underutilized by employees include participation in tax-deferred savings plans such as 401(k)s, inappropriate health plan elections and failure to take advantage of flexible spending accounts.

Consider This:

In a 2005 survey of retirement savings patterns conducted by the Employee Benefit Research Institute (EBRI), nearly 40% of eligible workers did not participate in employment-based retirement plans!

Even more alarming is that about half the workers who do participate have less than $25,000 in their plans, and 60% of workers have never tried to calculate how much they need to save for retirement.[2] **Exhibit 5-1** highlights how much workers reported having saved for retirement in the 2005 EBRI retirement savings survey.[3] When reviewing this exhibit, how do your retirement savings stack up? In order to attain financial wellness, most people will need much more retirement savings than shown in **Exhibit 5-1** set aside to pay for the ongoing expenses associated with retirement.

Exhibit 5-1—Total Worker Savings and Investments (Not Including Value of Primary Residence)

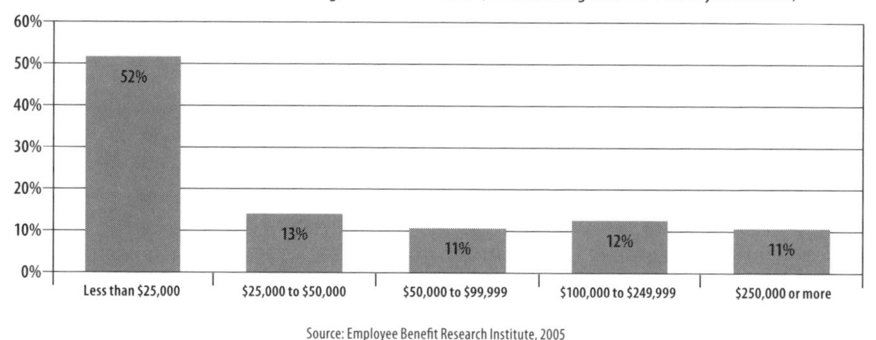

Source: Employee Benefit Research Institute, 2005

Use 401(k)-Type Plans To Achieve Financial Wellness

The best worksite vehicles for building financial wellness are 401(k), 403(b), or 457 plans, or any IRS qualified plan that allows you to make pre-tax payroll contributions to your retirement account. For this chapter, 401(k) plans will serve as our reference point for review. However, if you are covered by a 403(b) plan *(offered by non-profit organizations)* or a 457 plan *(offered by governmental organizations)* the principles of saving and growth discussed for 401(k) plans will also apply to you.

As an incentive to participate in the employer-sponsored plan, most organizations will offer some level of matching contribution for pre-tax contributions made by employees. Failure to take advantage of the full amount of a company's matching contribution is like "leaving money on the table!" Matching contributions represent an instant return on your investment, and often any matching funds received by an employer are immediately vested (owned) by the employee. Employer matching contributions represent the best investment return most people will ever earn without taking undue financial risk.

Consider This:

Let's say, for example, that your employer offers a 25% matching contribution in your company savings program, up to 10% of your pay. For every dollar you put in your plan up to 10% of pay, you are actually receiving a 25% rate of return! Some employers will contribute even more for matching contributions, which further serves to increase your investment return. The lesson: Do everything possible to contribute up to your company's matching contribution.

Payroll deduction is one of the best methods to save for retirement. When payroll deduction is used, saving for retirement is convenient, automatic, and after a few paychecks have passed, most people generally don't miss the money that is flowing into their retirement plans. If you have 15 or more years before retirement, a good guideline to follow for saving through an employer plan is to devote at least 10% of your total earnings to your plan. If both you and your spouse are employed, each of you should contribute at least 10% of your earnings. When your timeframe is less than 15 years, you may need to save even more to have enough funds available for a financially solid retirement.

Not sure how much you should save for retirement? Consider using a retirement calculator to keep you on track for building appropriate retirement funds. You can find a variety of retirement calculators on the Internet by going to a search engine (like Google or Yahoo) and typing in key words: *retirement planning calculator.* One retirement calculator I'd recommend can be found on the Bloomberg.com website. The address for this calculator is: bloomberg.com/invest//calculators/retire.html. Within a matter of minutes, a good retirement calculator will provide you with an analysis of how much you'll need to put aside to provide a solid retirement. I recommend using a retirement calculator on an annual basis. The reason for this is that your financial picture will change from year to year, and it's a good idea to make sure your level of retirement savings are keeping pace with the projected expenses you'll have in retirement.

An Easy Way To Increase 401(k)-Type Plan Savings—The 1% Concept

What if saving 10% or more of your total earnings is too much of a stretch for you to put into your 401(k)-type plan? First, if there is a company match, do everything possible to at least set aside enough to get the full amount of the company match.

Then every time you get a raise, commit to increasing your 401(k) contribution by just 1% with each raise received. For example, if you get a 3% raise, contribute 1% (⅓ of your raise) to your 401(k) plan. Since most of us receive annual pay increases, a 1% increase in 401(k) savings each year can really add up over a period of a few years. And the best part to this strategy is that you increase your contribution when you have additional dollars available as a result of a pay increase.

Contributing to a 401(k) is made easy through the convenience of payroll deduction. With payroll deduction, your contributions are made automatically into your account. Regardless of the direction of financial markets, your automatic 401(k) contribution takes away the stress of trying to find the best time to invest in the financial markets. When market prices are high, you buy fewer shares of stock and fewer bonds (usually through mutual fund investments). On the flipside, when market prices fall, you automatically purchase more stocks and bonds. *That's the magic of "dollar-cost averaging."* This method keeps your money working in all types of financial markets and allows you to avoid getting caught up trying to time your contributions to match the inevitable price changes in financial markets. (Note: dollar-cost averaging does not guarantee that you'll earn a positive return on your investments.)

Avoid These Top 401(k) Mistakes

Once you've started systematic investment in your 401(k), your account balances will start an upward path of growth over a period of time. With any type of investment plan, time is your greatest asset in dealing with the inevitable ups and downs of financial markets. To give you the best shot at achieving financial wellness, avoid these common mistakes when investing in your 401(k) or company savings program:

- **Avoid changing your investment strategy based on the "direction" of the financial markets.** Pick an appropriate mix of stock and bond mutual fund investments offered by your employer and stick with your plan. Don't try to time the market. Research has shown that it can't be done consistently. Investors who time the market earn lower returns than those who invest for the long run by keeping fully invested in all market cycles. Consider making adjustments to your plan only once per year. By making adjustments on an annual basis, you accomplish a "rebalancing" of your portfolio, allowing you to keep an appropriate mix of investments based on your goals, risk tolerance and age. This will allow you to ride out the volatility of financial markets and to adjust your portfolio in a planned, systematic fashion.

- **Avoid contributing below the point of any employer matching contribution.** This is free money to you when you save enough to take advantage of your employer's matching contribution. Think of it as a way to vote yourself a pay increase. All you need to do is develop the discipline to save at least enough to capture your employer's entire match.

- **Avoid being too conservative or too aggressive with your investment allocation.** Here's a good benchmark to consider when allocating your investments between stocks and bonds. This asset allocation benchmark involves subtracting your current age from 120. The result is the approximate percentage you should devote to stocks or stock mutual funds, with the balance being allocated to more conservative investments like bonds or bond mutual funds. So, if you're 40 years old, a diversified mix of about 80 percent stock mutual funds and 20 percent bond mutual funds is prudent for most people. There are many exceptions to this general rule, however, so make sure your investment mix is appropriate for your age, income, and objectives. The advice of a competent financial planner can be invaluable in helping you to determine the appropriate asset allocation for your unique circumstances.

- **Avoid plan loans.** Some plans allow loans to participants for a variety of purposes. By taking out a plan loan, you are compromising the growth of your plan over time. If you leave or lose your job, the loan must be repaid generally within 60 days following termination. Failure to repay the entire loan balance within this time frame will make your outstanding loan balance subject to income taxes and a 10% penalty (for those under the age of 59 ½).[4] Even if you don't lose your job, loans must be repaid within five years to avoid these harsh penalties.

- **If possible, avoid having more than 10% of your employer's stock in your account.** Think of Lucent Technologies, Enron and a host of other companies that have either gone out of business or have seen their stock price crushed by changing business conditions. Retirees lost their retirement security, while current employees lost both their jobs and their retirement security. If you work for an employer that makes its stock available, limit your financial exposure to less than 10% of your retirement account value. If you have significantly more than 10% of your assets in company stock, you are probably taking on too much financial risk. In some cases, (especially with employer profit sharing plans) you may have more than 10% of employer stock in your account due to employer contributions of company stock. In these situations, make sure you know your options for selling employer stock.

- **Avoid cashing out of your plan when leaving employment.** Cashing out is easy to do if you've accumulated only a few thousand dollars. By cashing out your 401(k) balance, you'll pay taxes and penalties and forego the tax-deferred returns you could have earned. Over half of those eligible to receive a lump sum distribution from a prior employer chose to use funds for current consumption, resulting in taxation of the distribution and tax penalties for early distribution of retirement proceeds.[5]

- **Avoid taking possession of your 401(k) proceeds and transferring them to a new employer or a rollover plan.** If you receive a check for your 401(k) balance, your employer must withhold 20% of the amount for federal income taxes. Even if you rollover your total amount within the IRS required 60 days following distribution, you'll still be responsible for coming up with the withheld 20% on your own to avoid paying income taxes and penalties. To avoid this headache, instruct your former employer to make a *direct transfer* to your new employer's plan or new rollover account vendor. By doing this, you avoid withholding taxes and penalties. Never take possession of a 401(k) plan distribution which you intend to roll into a different 401(k) plan or an IRA. The risk of incurring severe penalties is too high.

- **Avoid leaving 401(k) proceeds with a former employer.** You will have many more options for your 401(k) proceeds by choosing a rollover IRA. Virtually every financial institution in the U.S. (banks, mutual fund companies, stock brokerage firms, etc.) offers an IRA rollover option for 401(k) plans. Remember to choose wisely when making any rollover. You have literally thousands of options for finding professionally managed mutual funds. A good source for locating excellent mutual funds for stocks and bonds can be found at Fidelity Investment's website, www.fidelity.com. Click on the fund updates section and you'll receive detailed analysis on over a thousand top mutual funds by category. Fidelity uses Morningstar's ranking system to provide a snapshot of the fund's performance. Morningstar is widely respected for its ranking of mutual fund performance.[6] Another way to search for mutual funds is to enter in an Internet search engine key words: *mutual fund selection*. This will provide you with a number of sites to review for fund consideration.

A New Option—The Roth 401(k)

A spin off of the Roth IRA is the Roth 401(k). This plan option was made available to employers with 401(k) plans beginning 1-1-06. Initially, few employers offered this option because it was scheduled to expire on December 31, 2010. However, the Pension Reform Act of 2006 removed the expiration date for Roth 401(k) plans, making Roth 401(k)s permanent options for 401(k) participants.[7] Look for this option to become available at more organizations. A key benefit of the Roth 401(k) is that there are no income maximums to consider for participation, unlike the Roth IRA. If a Roth 401(k) option is made available at your worksite, consider placing at least a portion of your 401(k) contributions in this account. Sure, you'll lose the tax-deductibility associated with your contributions, but you'll never have to pay income taxes on distributions from your Roth 401(k) during retirement. It is likely that over the next few years, the Roth 401(k) will become a mainstream option in a considerable number of employer-sponsored 401(k) plans.

Ignore The Experts—Consistently Invest In Financial Markets

When you listen to financial experts discuss their personal observations about financial markets, you'll hear a variety of predictions regarding the financial markets' next move. For every market optimist there is a market pessimist. In financial lingo, there are always market "bulls," who are optimistic about financial markets, and market "bears," who are pessimistic about the direction of the financial markets.

Consider This:

Does the following sound familiar? You listen to one respected personal finance show and you are convinced that you should sell all your financial assets because a financial market "expert" has convinced you that the next big financial market "crash" is just around the corner. But, before acting on this expert's opinion, you decide to tune into another personal finance show and the featured "expert" makes you feel as though you should immediately invest every dime you have in the financial markets "before you miss the next upward movement of the financial markets." The fact of the matter is that no one knows the future direction of financial markets. Got that? No one, not even the pros can consistently call the financial markets' next movement.

Events that drive financial markets are simply too complex for any individual or organization to fully understand over any period of time, especially over a period of several months, with reliable accuracy. Sure, some experts will call the next financial market move right on target, but research has shown they are equally likely to be dead wrong on future market movements. **Making consistently correct predictions about the direction of financial markets is a demonstration of luck, not expertise.**

Does the daily conflicting advice from financial experts sound familiar and leave you a bit frustrated about what to do in financial markets? Understand this: Fear and greed often drive financial markets in the short-term. Since you more than likely will have years before you'll need the proceeds from your investments, understand that the sometimes volatile ups and downs of financial markets creates the environment you'll need to secure long-term investment gains. *Always remember that your basic human nature that fears "loss" is your biggest liability to long-term gains in financial markets.* Choose a solid long-term investment strategy and stick with it during all financial market phases.

Mutual Funds Are Best For Most Investors

I've followed the financial markets for over 25 years and have significant stock and bond holdings (mainly in mutual funds) that I've accumulated over the past two decades of investing. One thing I know for sure is that no one can accurately predict the future direction of financial markets. That's why it's vitally important to choose investments for the long-term and simply ignore the "noise" associated with the daily movement of financial markets and the so called "expert" predictions of the financial markets' next big movement.

For most people, and for most participants in employer-sponsored retirement plans, the best way to invest for long-term goals is through properly diversified mutual funds. Mutual funds offer professional management and eliminate the complexities an individual encounters when selecting individual securities. Individual stock and bond selection is difficult for most investors. Unless you have an advanced understanding of stock markets and considerable time to devote to individual stock tracking, stay clear of individual stock or bond selections and invest most of your retirement savings in mutual funds.

How Mutual Funds Work

Mutual funds for stocks and bonds purchase a variety of securities inside each fund, serving to lower the risk associated with any one investment performing poorly. This is the principle behind *diversification*. Mutual funds offer investors instant diversification through the holding of many different securities in the mutual fund portfolio. Chances are your 401(k) has a number of mutual fund options for your consideration. *Make sure that you take the time to understand the differences among the funds. If you go to the fund sponsor's website, you can find descriptions of each fund's profile, objectives, major holdings, annual expenses, and so on.*

A prospectus is a 25-75 page document that defines how the mutual fund will invest your hard-earned dollars. Each mutual fund has a stated objective and the prospectus will define how the mutual fund will operate to achieve the fund's stated objective. You may find some of the information contained in a prospectus insightful, but a normal prospectus is often very difficult to read and understand.

No matter how you do it—through an on-line site or from a prospectus—make sure you understand how the mutual fund will invest your money and consider the types of investments that the fund owns.

Standard Deviation Measures Risk

Look for a mutual fund that has a solid record of returns over a period of years. Also understand the "risk" of the mutual fund. Risk is measured by a statistical term called *standard deviation*. Standard deviation measures how much an investment can vary from its average return. When you see a high standard deviation, the investment's risk is high and expect that annual returns will fluctuate by quite a wide margin. Typically standard deviations are much higher for stock versus bond mutual funds. Growth-oriented stock mutual funds usually have higher standard deviations than value-oriented stock mutual funds. Standard deviations for bond funds can also vary considerably. Long-term bond funds will have much higher standard deviations than short-term bond funds.

So does that mean you should only select mutual funds with low standard deviations? Absolutely not. *Risk and return are inseparable.* Most of us want the highest return possible with an appropriate level of risk. The key to getting the best return is to carefully evaluate the risk you are taking when investing in a mutual fund. Since most people won't need 401(k) money for a period of several years, time is definitely the best weapon to reduce the impact of a fund's standard deviation. With more time to invest, annual fluctuations in investment returns fall more in line with long-term averages, resulting in an offsetting of stellar, positive annual returns and negative annual returns. In other words, the longer you own stocks, the lower the risk (measured by the standard deviation). *Remember with any type of investing, you need to have your mind focused on the long-haul—and the long-haul is measured in years, not months.*

Health Plan Selection

The most radical changes in employer-sponsored benefits have and will continue to occur with health insurance plans. Why? Cost increases have grown at an absolutely staggering pace since 2000. **Exhibit 5-2** shows the growth of health insurance premiums relative to workers' wages and overall inflation. Health insurance premiums have been growing at a multiple of these two benchmarks at a time when businesses of all sizes have been unable to pass along price increases to customers to compensate for higher insurance premiums. The result has been more cost shifting to employees. While healthcare costs continue to rise, health plan benefits continue to shrink, with higher deductibles, coinsurance and more complexity in how to navigate the healthcare system to maximize health plan benefits. Although the annual rate of increase in health insurance premiums has been trending down since peaking in 2003, premiums remain at levels that are alarming to both businesses and consumers. The future also promises a continuation of escalating health insurance premium increases due to a variety of factors, including the rise in individual obesity levels and the relentless demand individuals have for the latest treatment options in pharmacy benefits and professional (physician and hospital) services.

For service businesses, the cost of health benefits is often the second highest expense, just below the cost of wages. Starbucks spent about 200 million on health insurance for its U.S. based employees in 2005. This is more than it spent on the coffee that it serves to its customers in the U.S.[8] Manufacturers also feel the brunt of high benefit expenses. General Motors Corporation (GM) spends more on health insurance for its employees and retirees than it spends on steel for the vehicles it manufactures![9] The health insurance cost for the 1.2 million employees, dependents and retirees GM covers adds about $1,200 to every vehicle sold. To remain competitive, organizations of all sizes need to look for ways to provide the best level of benefits at a cost that will keep the organization competitive in the global economy in which we compete.

Exhibit 5-2—Health Insurance Premiums Are Skyrocketing

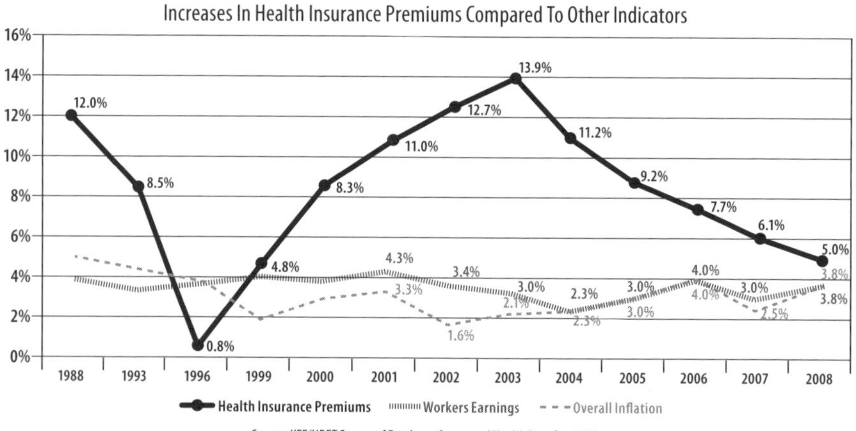

Source: KFF/HRET Survey of Employer-Sponsored Health Benefits: 2008

Health Insurance—The Future

Moving forward, there is good news and bad news for both employers and employees regarding health insurance. The good news is that as consumers we will have more choices in how we will pay for and receive healthcare services. Look for options like Health Reimbursement Accounts (HRAs) and Health Savings Accounts (HSAs) to be offered. These accounts are like 401(k) plans for healthcare expenses. Certain health expenses not covered by your health insurance plan can be paid from the HRA or HSA on a tax-free basis. HRA and HSA plans fall under the general category of "Consumer-Directed" healthcare plans. These plans give you more choice in choosing healthcare providers and healthcare services and combine health insurance with a savings account used to pay for eligible medical expenses not covered by your health insurance policy.

The bad news associated with health insurance is that it is going to continue to cost you and your employer considerably more in the years ahead.

Consider This:

In a December 2006 article published in the respected Journal of the American Medical Association, *total healthcare costs now consume more than 10 percent of the family income of nearly 50 million Americans under the age of 65!*

The movement toward Consumer-Directed healthcare is starting to take hold across the nation, as employers are seeking to make healthcare expenses more affordable and to involve employees in the ultimate cost and the appropriate use of health insurance. The potential reward for some employees is lower health insurance premiums and costs when healthcare services are used appropriately. The movement to a consumer-based model for delivery and payment of health insurance represents a shift from defined benefit healthcare financing to defined contribution financing for healthcare expenses. Note that this shift to defined contribution healthcare follows the shift that has occurred with pension plans from defined benefit plans to defined contribution 401(k)-type plans.

Understand Your Health Benefit Options

It is absolutely essential that you understand your employer's health benefit options. Mistakes when using healthcare services are seldom inexpensive and can create a huge hole in your budget.

Be sure to attend employer-organized open enrollment meetings and ask questions to clarify health plan benefit options. *Take the time to carefully read all open enrollment materials so that you understand the options that are available for your health benefits.* Also be sure to take into account the unique health needs of family members who will be covered under your plan. Since many employers offer more than one health plan choice, carefully consider how much each plan will cost you in premium payments, deductibles, and co-payments and determine whether it makes sense to pay more for a plan that offers enhanced benefits.

Don't overlook the underlying "network" of participating providers when choosing a plan. The best place to start is to find out if your family doctor or a good number of doctors close to work or your home participate in the insurer's plan. If the doctors you'd normally use are not in the insurer's network, you'll pay more when you receive health services from them, because the doctors do not participate with the insurer and will often charge much more than the insurer will pay. In addition, most insurers will assess a financial penalty (by paying reduced benefits and assessing higher deductibles) when you use a provider who does not participate in the insurer's network. The quality of the health insurer's participating provider network (which consists of physicians and hospitals) will have a significant impact on your satisfaction with the health plan.

Make Good Health A Priority

Take the time to optimize your health. Get regular exercise, proper rest and routine physical exams. Find out if your employer is offering financial incentives to encourage healthful lifestyle changes. If so, take advantage of these incentive programs that will generally result in real financial savings to you and improved health if you choose to follow the recommendations of your healthcare provider. Take the time to ask your healthcare provider questions about ways to improve your overall health. The adage: *"When you're healthy you're wealthy"* will ring true as healthcare expenses will continue to shift more to the employee and especially to those who use healthcare services the most. Those who utilize healthcare appropriately and make proper lifestyle decisions stand to have the best financial outcome in the upcoming era of consumer financial responsibility for healthcare.

Pay Attention To Your Health And Get Rewarded

Employers and employees cannot continue to pay double-digit health insurance rate increases that have been prevalent for the past few years. Since most employees pay some portion of the health insurance premium (on average, about 25%), employees are feeling the squeeze of both higher insurance premiums and less plan benefits. Something has to give to keep health insurance premiums affordable. Although no one can say with any level of precision what the health insurance environment will look like a decade from now, it is reasonable to assume that anyone who has employer-based coverage will be rewarded through lower premiums, better health plan benefits and financial incentives for practicing good health behaviors. Why? Health behaviors drive approximately

50% of all healthcare costs.[10] **Exhibit 5-3** illustrates four key factors that drive individual healthcare costs. This chart shows the impact our health behaviors have on our overall health, well-being and on healthcare costs.

Exhibit 5-3—Determinants Of Individual Health

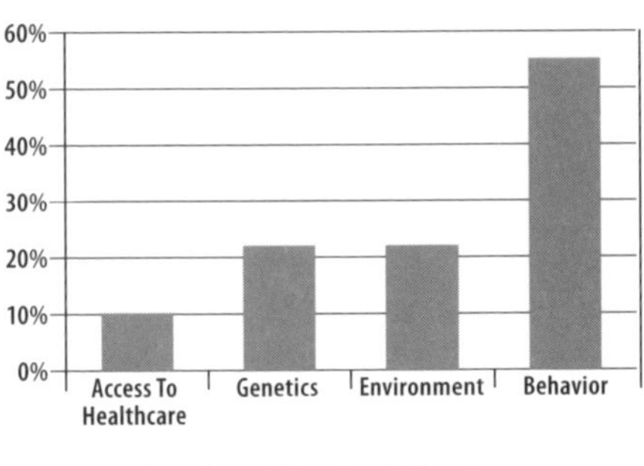

Source: Centers For Disease Control & Prevention

Many employers are now offering both financial incentives and financial penalties for health behaviors related to smoking, alcohol use, seat belt usage and failure to enroll in disease and lifestyle management programs when individual risk factors indicate a high probability for disease or illness. Lifestyle management programs are designed to help those with diabetes, elevated body-mass index, high blood pressure, high total cholesterol, elevated blood sugar and a host of other manageable conditions improve their overall health and lower healthcare use for treatment of the condition. Employers and employees alike are coming to the realization that lifestyle choices are a major factor in overall healthcare costs and are beginning to charge those who embrace healthful lifestyle practices less for health insurance. This makes good business sense and results in a financial incentive (through lower premiums or better plan benefits) for good health behaviors.

Health insurers are also starting to recognize the link that health behaviors have on overall healthcare costs and are beginning to reward those who have either excellent health or are actively working to improve personal health. Insurers are beginning to offer better health plan benefits to those members who demonstrate compliance with stated plan requirements.[11] The result is often better benefits at the same or lower cost than benefits offered to those who choose not to comply with the terms of the insurer's health and lifestyle management programs. Find out if your health plan or employer offers incentives for participation in health risk assessments (which give you a snapshot of your overall health status) and for practicing specified health and lifestyle choices. Usually participation in programs that improve health make good personal sense and often require modest effort for the potentially huge payoff in improved long-term health, a prerequisite for overall financial wellness.

Understand And Take Advantage Of Voluntary Benefits

Due to the cost of benefits, more and more employers are making a number of worksite benefits "voluntary" in nature. What this means is that employees need to decide whether to take coverage in the voluntary program (and pay for the benefit) or decline the offered benefit. Voluntary programs vary from employer to employer, but common benefits that fall under the voluntary benefit umbrella include life insurance, vision benefits, dental coverage, disability policies and a variety of other benefits offered under "cafeteria plans." Not all benefits fit each employee's needs, but make sure you understand how the voluntary benefit could impact you. Employers often secure attractive pricing from companies offering voluntary coverage, so you will often find that, if you need the coverage, it makes sense to enroll in voluntary plan offerings.

Know Your Options At Open Enrollment

Usually voluntary benefits are offered for consideration once each year during an employer's annual "open enrollment" period. Open enrollment periods generally last one or two weeks to give employees time to assess the benefit options that work best for them. Make sure that you devote the necessary time to understand the benefit options offered and the choices you'll need to make. *If you fail to enroll during open enrollment and subsequently wish to take coverage, you'll more than likely need to wait until the next annual open enrollment period to enroll in the program.* This can prove costly if you need the benefit before the next date for enrollment.

Consider Enrollment In "Flexible Spending" Accounts

Find out if your employer offers a "flexible spending account" (FSA) for medical expenses. If you have children in daycare, also determine whether there is a flexible spending account for daycare expenses. You may wish to consult IRS Publication 503 (www.irs.gov) for detailed information or search the Internet for easier-to-understand descriptions about qualified dependent care expenses. Use of these spending accounts can save you at least 25% in payroll and income taxes, since these expenses are deducted from your pay on a pre-tax basis.

IRS publication 502 provides guidance on medical expenses that are qualified for payment from your flexible spending account (www.irs.gov). **Appendix 5-1** (located in the Appendix Section in the back of this book) shows the variety of medical expenses that can be paid from a flexible spending account during a plan year.[12] As you can see, the list includes most of the necessary healthcare expenses you are likely to incur.

However, the national average for enrollment in FSAs is only 18% of those employees eligible for coverage.[13] Why do so few employees take advantage of this benefit? The biggest reason is the *"use it or lose it"* provision that requires use of all FSA funds during the plan year. Any unused funds at the conclusion of the plan year are lost or forfeited to the employer. As a consequence, when you consider an FSA for medical expenses, make a conservative estimate of how much you will be spend on eligible medical expenses not covered by insurance. By taking just a few minutes to make this calculation (which can really add up), the medical expense FSA can be a great way to pay for medical expenses on a pre-tax basis. I've found that most employees can benefit from enrollment in a medical FSA plan. You'll get only one chance per year to take advantage of this key benefit due to IRS rules on enrollment. If you enroll in a FSA plan, your elected contributions cannot be changed during the plan year unless you have a "qualifying event." Qualifying events are defined as:

- **A birth of or an adoption of a child.**
- **Marriage, divorce or legal separation.**
- **Death of a covered individual.**
- **Child loses eligibility because of age or marriage.**
- **Employee's spouse gains or loses coverage through employment.**
- **Significant changes in health benefits provided by a spouse's employer.**

Take A Close Look At Your Healthcare Expenses

Because most health insurance plans require deductibles, coinsurance, higher copays for office visits and prescription drugs, the use of an FSA for medical expenses makes sense for most employees. Don't pass on participation in this excellent benefit without doing a calculation on how much you (and your covered dependents) will likely spend on eligible medical expenses not paid by your health insurance plan. Be sure to ask your benefits representative questions about this coverage prior to your enrollment. You'll be responsible for submitting documentation for all eligible expenses, typically to a third party claims administrator for verification and payment. To ensure payment for all covered expenses, be sure to set up a convenient file for FSA-related documentation. This will help you locate all necessary documentation (explanation of benefit forms from insurance carriers, receipts from medical providers, etc.) when it's time to submit your covered medical expenses for reimbursement.

Pulling It Together

Effectively utilizing benefits made available from your employer is the foundation for long-term financial wellness. By taking the vital steps listed in this chapter, you'll set into motion the awesome power of tax-deferred investment growth and you'll select the best health and ancillary benefits that complement your overall financial well-being. In the next chapter, we'll examine practical steps for saving and investing your hard-earned dollars outside of any company savings plans you may have.

Take the time to review and complete the *Action Step Checklist* on the following page. After completion of the *Checklist*, let's move on to **Step #6** and explore *Ideas for Saving and Investing...*

5
ACTION STEP CHECKLIST

Step #5 Action Step Checklist

Congratulations on completing Step #5. Listed are some key Action Steps to consider from this chapter. When you've finished the Action Step, place a ✓ next to the Step to document your progress.

Here is your Action Step Checklist from Step #5:

- ______Take a look at your savings options through your employer's plan. If your employer offers a matching contribution, make sure you take full advantage of matching contributions. Also look at your other options to build retirement savings, especially through IRA contributions. Remember that funding a secure retirement is your responsibility.

- ______Plan on Social Security and Medicare changing in the next few years. This means that Social Security benefits will likely be lower and premiums for Medicare coverage when you turn 65 will be significantly higher. This makes it crucial to save through available retirement account options.

- ______Avoid the top 401(k) mistakes listed in the chapter. Pick a mix of stock and bond mutual funds that is appropriate for your age. A basic way to choose a solid allocation between stocks and bonds is to subtract your age from 120. The result is the approximate allocation you will devote to stock mutual funds. The difference is usually allocated to bond mutual funds.

- ______Avoid cashing out your 401(k) if you leave your current employer prior to retirement. Instead, arrange a direct transfer of your 401(k) balance from your former employer to a Rollover IRA.

- ______Don't try to "out-smart" the financial markets. Ignore the financial experts' latest opinions on the future direction of financial markets. Long-term investing success is measured by good asset allocation and staying invested in the market at all times.

- ______Most people are best served by investing in mutual funds. Individual stock picking takes time and knowledge about individual companies. It also increases risk in most cases. Keep an eye on long-term mutual fund performance, and make sure you understand how the fund operates and its overall investment objective and fees.

- ______Health insurance premiums will continue to rise, and this will result in added cost and different plan options for your consideration. Take the time to know the plan options available to you through your employer. You may find that the plan with the highest deductible offers the best value. Also take advantage of any health incentives your employer may offer, as this will often lower your insurance cost and improve your health.

6

STEP 6
Ideas For Saving And Investing

"Save for today but invest for tomorrow."

Risk And Return Are Inseparable

A basic rule of personal finance is that in order to earn a higher return, you must take on a higher level of risk. **Exhibit 6-1** shows how the returns of investments are directly related to their underlying risk as measured by the standard deviation. Standard deviation is a way to evaluate the probability that an investment will deviate or vary from its expected return. Understand that the higher the standard deviation, the higher the risk.

Matching the level of risk with your financial objectives and level of comfort is critical for achieving long-term financial wellness. Not taking enough risk can result in low returns. Low risk investments include bank savings accounts, money market accounts and certificates of deposit. Sure these investments won't nosedive when other assets like stocks and bonds go into a tailspin. But they also won't increase significantly in value when stocks and bonds rise. Factor in the adverse impact of both inflation and income taxes, and in most years low risk investments will not keep pace with the long-term growth you'll need to build long-term financial wellness.

In this chapter, I'll focus primarily on financial assets and provide you with an overview of the types of financial asset classes you'll need to know to achieve long-term financial wellness. **Exhibit 6-2** shows how investments in stocks have been consistently the best place for investors from 1970 through 2004. But, over short periods of time, bonds and U.S. Treasury bills (for example, from 2000 through year 2004) can outperform stock investments.

Exhibit 6-1—Expected Asset Class Returns And Risk

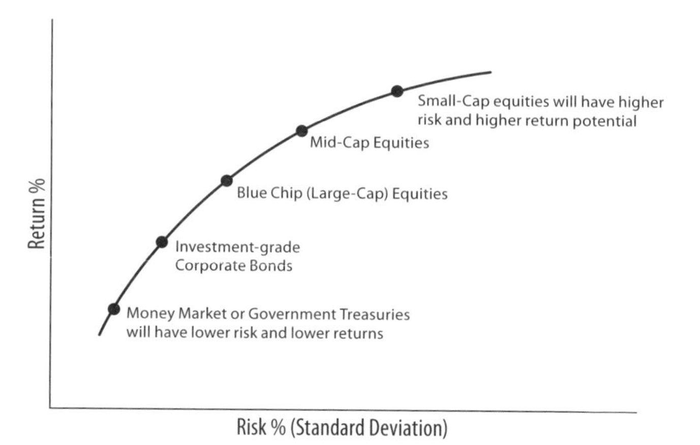

Exhibit 6-2—Average Annual Total Returns (As of 12/31/04) For Stocks, Bonds And Treasury Bills

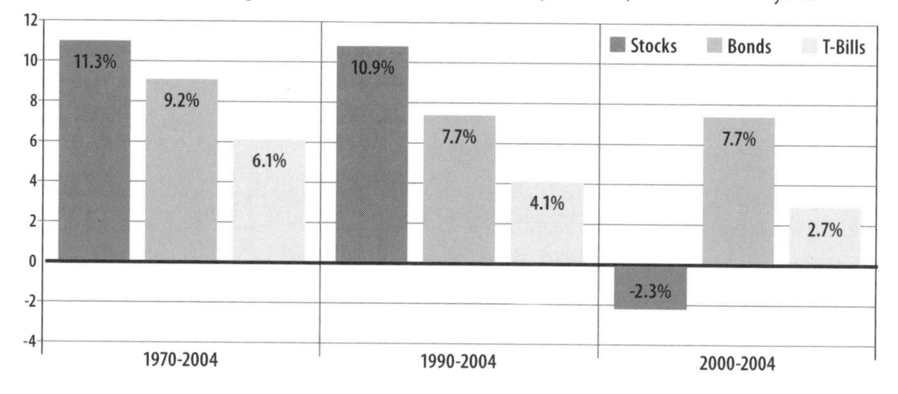

Source of chart data: Standard & Poor's Micropal Inc. Stocks are represented by the S&P 500 Index, a widely used measure of U.S. stock market performance, bonds by the Lehman Aggregate Bond Index, and T-bills by a 91-day Treasury Bill Index. For the 1970-2004 periods, bonds are represented by S&P Long-term Government Bonds.

Since real estate is the most significant investment most people have (through the purchase of their own home), we'll also discuss investment in real estate for personal use and for investment purposes. In order to properly understand the risk inherent in every investment, you must understand the elements that drive risk. Time is one of the most important risk reduction strategies for most long-term investments. Generally, the longer you hold an investment, the lower your risk will be. This is especially true with investments in stocks, which can be very risky over short periods of time. But, with a multi-year timeframe, stock investments (primarily through well-diversified mutual funds) will often provide the best overall opportunity for the growth needed to attain financial wellness. Let's now examine the basic asset classes for consideration.

Cash Investments—Great For Emergency Funds & Short-Term Needs

So called "cash investments" are the least risky investments you can make over short periods of time. Checking accounts, savings accounts, money market accounts, short-term certificates of deposit and U.S. Treasury Bills fall into the broad category of cash investments.

Everyone should have a short-term emergency fund that can be quickly tapped to fund unexpected expenses due to a major repair, unexpected illness or loss of a job. The absolute minimum amount you should have set aside for your personal financial emergency fund is three months' of anticipated unavoidable living expenses. The ideal level of emergency funding will allow for six months' of living expenses. Since an emergency fund should be used only for true emergencies, you need to have your investments in safe, short-term accounts that won't fluctuate in value and will be readily available on short-term notice when you need access to your money. For most people, placing money in a savings account or money market account is the perfect place for emergency fund money or for money to pay for expenses that they know they'll have coming due within a short period of time. *Cash investments provide much needed "liquidity" to help us pay current and unexpected expenses.*

A good source for finding the best short-term rates can be found at Bankrate.com (www.bankrate.com). By using this website, you can quickly find competitive rates for savings accounts, checking accounts and money market accounts in both your area and across the U.S. Establishing a short-term emergency fund should be the first step you take (after paying off credit card debt) on your path to long-term financial wellness. With sufficient cash-type assets in your emergency fund, you'll provide yourself with the necessary flexibility you'll need to pay for unexpected expenses and to get you through short-term financial setbacks. Always try to rebuild your emergency fund as quickly as possible if you've needed to use it. By having three to six months' of short-term financial reserves in your emergency fund, you should be able to proactively pursue longer-term financial goals.

Make Bond Investments Part Of Your Long-Term Portfolio

Bond investments certainly don't have the excitement or the ability to produce the types of long-term financial returns that you can get with stocks. However, bonds are an essential ingredient in most financial portfolios. Why? Because bonds offer much better long-term investment gains than "cash-type" investments, and they are a lot less volatile in the short run than stock investments. *Think of bonds as "shock absorbers" for financial markets.* Generally, when financial markets get bumpy, bonds will hold their value better than stocks.

Bonds are especially important to people who want guaranteed cash payments (generated by interest on their bonds) to supplement their retirement income. Most bonds pay interest twice each year; the same dollar amount year after year, no matter whether financial markets are strong or weak. That steady income promise makes bonds attractive to many retirees.

So how do you invest in bonds? For most people, the best way is through bond mutual funds. *Unless you have enough money and the expertise to buy bonds from several different issuers,* about the only type of single bond the average investor should buy direct is U.S. Savings Bonds. These bonds can be purchased sometimes through your employer via payroll deduction or at a local bank or credit union. You can even go direct to the U.S. Treasury website and purchase bonds directly at www.treasurydirect.gov. U.S. Savings Bonds are easy to purchase and can be part of a solid investment strategy for a long-term goal such as education (there is federal income tax relief when U.S. Savings bonds are used for qualified college expenses).

Series EE Bonds issued after May 2005 earn a fixed rate of interest and are issued at 50% of the bond's face value, with a minimum purchase of $50.[1] Series I ("I" denotes the word *inflation*) bonds are issued at 100% of the bond's face value. These bonds can be purchased in increments starting at $50.[2] However, unlike Series EE Bonds, Series I bonds adjust the interest rate paid twice per year to account for inflation. As a result, Series I bonds provide inflation protection, as the interest rate paid will increase when interest rates rise and fall when interest rates decline. Note that these bonds can be redeemed starting one year following purchase, but a three month interest penalty will apply to both Series EE and Series I Bonds when they are cashed in within 5 years of issue. These bonds will pay interest for a period of 30 years.

Why should the average investor stay away from single bond purchases outside of U.S. Savings Bonds? The reason is complexity and the market liquidity for most single bond investments. Some bonds (especially some municipal bonds) are not easy to buy and sell, resulting in decreased liquidity. As a result, you may end buying these bonds at a much higher price, or selling them at a much lower price, because the market for them is so small.

Also, many bonds are sold in denominations that start at $1,000 or even $5,000 increments, making individual bond purchases too expensive for the average investor. The solution to this dilemma is to buy bonds through well-diversified bond mutual funds. *Through bond mutual funds, you get professional management and you get the benefits of having a diversified portfolio of bond investments that serves to substantially lower investment risk when compared to buying bonds individually.*

When choosing a bond mutual fund or bond exchange traded fund, pay attention to annual fund expenses. You can find annual expenses listed in the bond mutual fund's prospectus or Internet site. A good rule to follow is to keep annual expenses in bond mutual funds below ½ of 1 percent.

Let's now take a look at some of the major bond classes you can purchase through mutual funds (or exchange-traded bond funds).

Short-Term Bond Funds

These funds offer the lowest level of interest rate risk for bond investments. Interest rate risk occurs when interest rates rise. As interest rates in the U.S. economy rise, the prices of all previously issued and still outstanding bonds will fall. As long as an investor holds the bonds to maturity, these price movements don't matter. The same dollars of interest are paid no matter what the bond's price is. But if bonds are to be sold prior to maturity—say, when long-term interest rates have risen—interest rate risk can be critical. In that case, bond investors will receive a lower price because of interest rate risk.

The shorter the bond portfolio's average annual maturity or duration, the less impact interest rate increases or decreases will have on the value of your investment.[3] Short-term bond portfolios typically have an overall maturity of between one and four years. Since a mutual fund often will hold hundreds of different bonds with differing short-term maturity dates, these funds are an excellent choice for investing if your timeframe for needing the funds is at least one to four years. See **Appendix 6-1**, Bond Mutual Fund Definitions (located in the Appendix Section in the back of this book) for a brief description of the most common types of bond mutual funds. These funds can be purchased as taxable funds or as tax-exempt municipal funds.

Intermediate-Term Bond Funds

These funds offer the *potential* for a higher returns than short-term bond funds due to their increased maturity (generally four to ten years), and therefore, higher risk. Interest rate changes have a bigger impact on the overall value of the fund over time. In a rising interest rate environment, these funds will generally lose value at a greater percentage than short-term funds. In a falling interest rate environment, these funds generally increase in value at a higher rate than short-term bond funds.

Long-Term Bond Funds

Long-term bond funds have an average maturity of 10 or more years. With a long-term average maturity, these funds are the most sensitive to interest rate changes. Unless your timeframe for needing the bond fund is 7 years or more, you should opt for the relative stability of short-term or intermediate bond funds in your portfolio. Although long-term bond funds offer the greatest risk of change when interest rates rise, understand that in a falling interest rate environment, investors in long-term bonds do exceptionally well, as these funds increase in value substantially in a falling interest rate environment. In addition, if bond funds are purchased to provide income at retirement and the intent is to hold the bonds until maturity, long-term bond funds are especially attractive. In that case, price instability due to fluctuating long-term interest rates in the U.S. economy is only a minor consideration.

Bond Terms to Know

When investing in bonds or bond mutual funds (including exchange traded bond funds), there is some basic terminology you should know to help you make the best decision on bond selection. Commonly used terms include:

- **Interest rate risk**—this is the risk that occurs when interest rates rise and fall. There is an inverse relationship between interest rates and bond values. The inverse—or opposite—relationship occurs as follows: *When interest rates rise, bond values fall. When interest rates fall, bond prices rise.* For most bond mutual funds, this is the biggest risk investors encounter because default risk has been minimized by the purchase of a substantial number of different bond securities, which lowers the impact of a given bond's default (default occurs when the bond fails to pay interest or principal due to financial distress, including bankruptcy by the bond's issuer).

- **Credit risk**—this type of risk is a component of every bond except U.S. Treasury obligations, which are backed by the faith and taxing power of the U.S. federal government. Credit risk (also known as default risk) is a primary concern when investing in "high-yield" bonds and bond mutual funds (sometimes referred to as junk bond funds). High-yield bond funds purchase junk, or more formally, non-investment grade bonds. Bond rating firms such as Standard & Poor's and Moody's assign ratings for bonds issued by corporations and governments. Standard & Poor's classifies a non-investment grade bond as one with a rating of BBB or lower; Moody's classifies a non-investment grade bond with a rating of Baa or lower.[4] Standard & Poor's classifies the highest rated bond investment at a rating of AAA; Moody's highest classification is Aaa. The lower a bond's rating, the higher the interest rate it must pay to attract investors. That's why a good bond rating from each of the major bond rating agencies is so important to organizations issuing bonds. A poor, or non-investment grade, rating results in the organization paying more when it issues bonds, as investors seek higher compensation for taking on more risk associated with higher odds of default.

- **Liquidity risk**—some bonds, especially municipal bonds, are not traded often or in large volume in financial markets. This can result in difficulty buying or selling a particular bond issue. Liquidity risk is one of the main reasons why mutual funds are the best way to invest in bonds for the average investor. In addition, brokerage commissions for bond trades can be quite steep, especially for bonds that are not actively traded. Commissions paid to a broker serve to lower your overall return.

Stock Investments: The Core Of Your Long-Term Investment Portfolio

Most investors lack the time, temperament or expertise to quickly build up their own diversified portfolio of individual stock investments. If you have the requisite qualities to invest successfully in individual stocks, make sure you purchase a variety of different stocks from different industry sectors, and be sure to have no more than 10% of the value of your stock investments concentrated in any one stock.

Consider DRIPs for Individual Stock Purchases

Let's say you want to invest in one or more individual stocks that you believe will perform well over a period of several years. There is a systematic and low cost way to do this for companies that pay ongoing dividends to their shareholders. A number of publicly traded companies offer investors Dividend Reinvestment Plans (DRIPs). Often to participate in a company's DRIPs, you need to own only one share of its stock. The big advantage is that when dividends are paid, your dividends automatically purchase more shares of the company's stock at the current market price without added commission. This can save you a bundle in brokerage fees over the years and also yield the corresponding benefit of accumulation of more company shares through dividend reinvestment. You will still pay current year income taxes on dividends reinvested in additional shares, but you will put those dividends to work by purchasing more stock.

Each company offering DRIPs sets its own rules for participation. Some companies will permit additional direct share purchases for cash without the use of a broker, called Direct Purchase Plans (DPPs).

You can find companies offering DRIPs online at: www.investorguide.com. This site lists companies that offer DRIPs to investors. If you are a frequent stock trader, DRIPs will likely not be a good choice for you. DRIPs reward long-term investors with the convenience of dividend reinvestment in additional company shares, and some plans allow for additional cash purchases of additional shares without brokerage fees. If you think DRIPs might be good for you, take the time to do your research on the companies offering them and the unique rules that each company sets for DRIPs participation. Understand that for most investors, DRIPs and individual stock purchases should not comprise the majority of stock holdings. Mutual funds and exchange traded funds work best for most stock purchases.

Stock Mutual Funds And Exchange Traded Funds Offer Diversification

Mutual funds and their related "cousins," exchange traded stock funds (ETFs), offer investors instant diversification. These funds invest in a variety of stocks (often 100 or more different companies), greatly reducing default risk associated with the bankruptcy of any of the component stocks. Mutual funds offer professional management and invest in all segments of the domestic and international stock markets. See **Appendix 6-2**, Stock Mutual Fund Definitions and **Appendix 6-3**, ETF Definitions (located in the Appendix Section in the back of this book) for a brief description of major types of funds. For mutual funds and ETFs, there are a variety of fund classifications, but for sake of simplicity, three of the most important fund classifications are listed below:

- **Large Capitalization Funds ("Large Caps")**—these funds invest primarily in stocks of companies with a market capitalization value that exceeds five billion dollars.[5] These funds tend to invest in the largest companies, most of which are household names such as Microsoft, Johnson & Johnson, General Electric, Wal-Mart, etc. Large capitalization funds can either be domestic or foreign in focus. The fund's prospectus (or Internet site) will provide you with the major investments contained in the fund.

- **Mid Capitalization Funds ("Mid Caps")**—these funds invest primarily in companies with a market capitalization between one billion to five billion dollars. Firms meeting these benchmarks typically have established businesses that may have opportunity for significant future growth. These funds can be either domestic or foreign in focus.

- **Small Capitalization Funds ("Small Caps")**—these funds typically invest in companies having a market capitalization under one billion dollars. Since small capitalization companies are much smaller than mid or large capitalization companies, they offer investors the opportunity for potentially larger growth, but can also carry more risk due to the size of these firms. (Remember, higher potential returns are possible only by taking higher risks.) These funds can also focus on domestic or foreign securities.

There are thousands of stock mutual funds and stock ETFs available that invest in a variety of industries, sectors of the economy, and follow a host of investment objectives (growth, value, blend, international, income, commodities, etc.). When investing in stock mutual funds, think variety and try to make sure that the core of your portfolio has both domestic and international funds that include stocks from the large, mid and small cap universe.

Picking Solid Stock Mutual Funds

As of April 2006, there were 8,606 mutual funds belonging to the Investment Company Institute (ICI), the national association of Investment Companies in the United States, with combined assets of $9.207 trillion dollars.[6] With so many choices and so many different types of mutual funds available, how do you find the best fund for your objectives? Here are some prudent steps you can take to identify quality mutual funds:

- **Look at long-term returns**—long-term returns are measured in 5 to 10 year segments. Compare the mutual fund to the benchmark it most closely follows. For example, most large capitalization stock funds compare their performance with the Standard & Poor's 500 Index. If the fund you are considering consistently performs better than the selected benchmark, it might be a good candidate for investment. The mutual fund's prospectus should provide this information to you along with other invaluable information about the structure and investment objectives of the fund. *Never invest in a mutual fund without first reviewing basic information about the fund from either the fund's prospectus or its Internet site.* A good independent source for mutual fund evaluation is Morningstar, Inc. This firm has developed the renowned Morningstar Rating System to rate the performance of mutual funds over a select period of years.[7] The Morningstar Rating System uses "stars" to rate the effectiveness of a mutual fund relative to similar mutual funds—its peers. One star is used for the lowest performing funds, and five stars for the best performing funds. Stick with funds that have earned a Morningstar Rating of at least 3 out of a possible 5 stars.

- **Assess fund fees**—the lowest fund fees can be found with index funds (for both stocks and bonds). Index funds are passively managed and attempt to track a particular segment of a bond or stock market such as the Standard & Poor's 500 Index, the Russell 2000 index of small companies, the Europe, Asia and Far East Index (EAFE) for foreign securities, etc. For personal investing, consider index funds for a percentage of your long-term investment portfolio. Their consistent returns, low income tax liability, and ultra-low management fees produce long-term after-tax returns eclipsing returns of most actively managed funds. As a rule of thumb, you should be able to find index funds charging annual fees of no more than ¼ of one percent of your portfolio value. Vanguard Investments brought index fund investing to the individual investor several years ago, and its lineup of index funds sets the industry standard for both breadth of funds and low fees. For more information about Vanguard's low-cost index funds, visit www.vanguard.com.

Higher fees are charged when mutual funds are actively managed. Sometimes the higher fund fee is worth it, especially if the fund has consistently beaten its benchmark index over a period of years. Note, however, that research shows you can't earn a higher return by selecting high-fee mutual funds. Instead, select a high-fee fund only if it has consistently out-performed its peer group of funds, and you expect that performance to continue.

Before investing in an actively managed fund find out how the fund has performed relative to its selected benchmark. If the fund has underperformed its targeted benchmark over a 5 or 10 year period, you should consider another fund. Limit your choice of domestic mutual funds to those with annual fees less than one percent. Keep annual international fund management fees below one and a half percent of your total asset value. Paying more than these guidelines for actively managed funds makes it difficult for the actively managed fund to outperform its targeted benchmark index over a period of years. *You can find ongoing mutual fund management fees listed either in the mutual fund's prospectus or on its Internet site.*

Thoughts On Stock Mutual Fund Selection

- **Avoid fund loads if selecting mutual funds on your own**—mutual funds are sold either with a "load" (or additional sales charge) or without a load (no-load). A sales load results in increased expense to you and serves to lower your investment return. *You should never pay a load if you select mutual funds without the advice and guidance of a financial advisor.* If you are working with a financial advisor, a load may be worth the additional cost, especially if your financial advisor provides you with ongoing guidance. American Funds, www.americanfunds.com, is one of the best fund families to use if you are working with a financial advisor. A number of American Funds have consistently outperformed their targeted financial benchmark over a period of years and their ongoing management fees are quite low compared to other managed mutual funds.

- **Don't chase returns**—invest for the long-term (measured in years) when making a stock mutual fund investment. Financial publications and mutual fund advertisements often feature the best performing funds over the past year. Often, these same funds will be the next year's bottom performing funds in the following year.

As a result, don't try to chase returns by investing in this year's top fund, unless it makes good sense. Investors who chase returns in this manner usually significantly underperform the market over time. Select solid mutual funds and hold them over time, unless something changes materially with the fund or your investment strategy.

- **Don't try to time the market**—this strategy rarely works consistently for anyone, including the stock market "experts." Remember your long-term financial wellness will be determined in a large part to "time in the market," not timing the market. Nobody knows for sure what the market will do today or tomorrow or next month. The best strategy is to choose your investment mix and stick with it over the long haul.

- **Consider lifecycle or target date funds for simplicity**—if you really want to simplify your investment strategy, consider investing in a lifecycle fund. These funds are offered by most major mutual fund companies. The investment manager in a lifecycle fund chooses a variety of stock and bond mutual funds from the fund's family for your lifecycle fund. The manager adjusts the mix of stock and bond investments to coincide with a "target date" when you will need to start drawing proceeds from the fund generally at retirement. Generally, the closer to retirement you get, the higher the proportion of your portfolio will be invested in bonds and relatively safe equity mutual funds. These types of funds offer one-stop shopping for the long-term investor. *Note that there is considerable variation in the asset allocation strategy of lifecycle fund managers.* Be sure to check the prospectus to ensure that the manager's allocation of stock and bond funds is appropriate for your investment goals.

Asset Allocation Is Crucial For Success

The whole idea behind asset allocation is to reduce risk through the selection of different asset classes, with the main classes being stocks, bonds and cash. With mutual funds and ETFs comprising the primary sources of financial investments for most people, diversification and asset allocation are easy to attain.

Consider This:

When it comes to investing, the most important decision you can make is the selection of the appropriate mix of investment types that will comprise your investment portfolio.

Proper asset allocation depends on the following two factors:

Two Key Factors For Proper Asset Allocation:

1. **Your age and timeframe**—You can take more risk the longer your investment time horizon. On the other hand, the sooner you will need to cash out your investments, the safer and more liquid they must be. This means that you will favor stock investments in the early stages of your investment time horizon and slowly purchase more bond investments (by reducing your stock investments) as your time horizon for needing the investment proceeds shortens.

2. **Your tolerance for risk**—If the thought of your investments losing value over an extended period of time—months or even years—keeps you from sleeping at night, you'll definitely want to invest more conservatively than someone who understands that losses in a stock mutual fund can be quickly made up when financial markets turn positive. A more aggressive tolerance for risk will result in a higher allocation to stock investments. A more conservative mindset will favor a more balanced approach to investing, with bonds and bond funds having a greater weight in a portfolio.

Through asset allocation you are dividing your portfolio among a variety of investment classes (primarily stock and bond classes), and as a result, you minimize your reliance on the performance of any one class. Some assets may experience growth while others decline. Because changing economic and financial conditions affect various types of assets differently, each asset category's return partially offsets those of others. Through proper asset allocation, these offsetting movements may reduce the overall risk of your portfolio and enhance returns. The effect of asset allocation is to make investment returns less volatile without sacrificing a significant reduction in long-term returns.

How effective is asset allocation? Ibbotson Associates, a respected leader in asset allocation education for investors, compiled data from research performed by Brinson, Hood and Beebower (1986) and Brinson, Singer and Beebower (1991) related to the importance of asset allocation on overall portfolio performance. *They found that over 90% of portfolio performance is explained by asset allocation.*[8] This study and scores of others examining the impact of proper asset allocation demonstrate the positive impact asset allocation has in the overall performance of an investment portfolio. *The lesson with asset allocation is to put your "investment eggs" in several baskets to reduce risk and to make stocks and bonds the cornerstone of your long-term investment strategy.*

Rebalance Your Portfolio Once Each Year For Proper Asset Allocation

Rebalancing goes hand-in-hand with asset allocation. Once appropriate asset allocation is achieved, it is important to make sure that the appropriate mix of stocks, bonds and cash remains in "balance" over time. *Most financial planners recommend rebalancing once per year.* Remember to include all accounts you have (both personal and retirement) when rebalancing. Rebalancing all of your investment accounts once per year ensures that your portfolio keeps your targeted balance of stock and bond percentages close to your investment objective for each asset class. When you do this, you also reduce portfolio risk and enhance return by selling assets that have increased in value (selling high) and increasing your exposure to other assets when their prices are low (buying low).

Consider This:

Rebalancing also serves to keep in check one of your biggest liabilities when investing: *emotions*. By sticking with your chosen asset allocation mix of bonds and stocks, the act of rebalancing allows for a systematic, unemotional way to bring your investment portfolio into balance with your long-term objectives.

Rebalancing Keeps Asset Allocation On Target With Your Investment Objectives

Since stock and bond values rise and fall, periodic rebalancing ensures that your asset allocation remains on target. Ibbotson Associates' research confirms the futility of trying to time the market by adjusting a portfolio to reflect short-term fluctuations in stock and bond prices. By following this time-tested strategy, you'll reduce your anxiety when stocks and bonds move up or down, and you'll take advantage of the long-term gains that financial markets deliver to investors who stay invested over a period of years. Remember that investing in "get rich quick" schemes don't work and that most successful investors choose a simple investment strategy, make few adjustments throughout the year, and as a result, enjoy the long-term growth of stocks helping them to achieve financial wellness.

Real Estate Investments

Many individuals include real estate in their investment portfolios. So does that mean that you should go out and buy real estate as an investment? It depends. If you are a homeowner, chances are the value of your home may be more than the value of all of your financial investments. If this is the case, you should probably stay away from direct real estate investments such as limited partnerships in real estate projects or buying real estate and becoming a landlord.

As a current owner of three duplex residential rental properties, I have found these to be decent investments. But I really underestimated the amount of time it would take to properly manage the properties. Sure, professional property managers are available, but they charge a handsome fee for their services, and the responsibility for the properties you buy is ultimately yours. *Outside of the purchase of your own home, you should avoid direct investment in real estate unless you have the time and expertise to select and manage properties over a period of years.* Contrary to the real estate investor "millionaire infomercials" on television, most people don't make huge investment returns when buying real estate for investment purposes. Also understand that any direct investment in real estate compromises your investment "liquidity." It can take years to sell certain properties, especially if the real estate market is in a downward price spiral. This can result in your money being literally "buried" in an investment that you cannot quickly sell at a reasonable price.

Consider A REIT For Real Estate Investments

Some mutual funds invest only in real estate. They are called Real Estate Investment Trusts (REITs—rhymes with "eats"), and these can be a good way to realize the advantages of real estate income and appreciation through the purchase of a professionally managed fund of real estate properties. Like all mutual fund investments, be sure to read the prospectus to know the type of REIT in which you are investing because no two REITs are the same. Most focus on income from the rents charged for properties. The property portfolio may consist of such diverse holdings such as apartments, office buildings, malls, resorts, warehouses, etc. In short, know what you are investing in and look at the long-term investment record of the REIT.

Accumulating wealth in real estate is similar in many respects to wealth accumulation in the stock market. It takes time and effort to attain significant wealth in both. Further, potential real estate riches involving direct investment in real estate can be risky business for the undercapitalized and the uninformed, passive investor. *Just remember, if you are in a red-hot real estate market, the law of gravity will apply, often when you least expect it.* When real estate markets have rapid, eye-popping gains, understand that there will come a time when the reverse is true for the same markets. Speculation drives all markets (financial and real estate) to sometimes illogical levels. Be careful not to get caught in a real estate bubble. All bubbles eventually burst, and the greediest investors typically get their just reward when the market quickly reverses direction.

Owning A Home

Chapter 3 highlights the advantages of home ownership and financing options. For most people, home ownership is one of the best financial moves they can make and will serve as a key "pillar" to building long-term financial wellness. Home ownership provides a number of both tangible and intangible benefits.

The tax deductibility of both mortgage interest and property taxes effectively serves to lower the true cost of home ownership. In addition, price appreciation over time bodes well for homeowners. Home ownership also results in a form of "forced savings" when mortgage payments reduce the principal balance of the loan, resulting in equity growth in a home.

Home equity is increased in two ways: when debt is reduced through each mortgage payment (assuming the loan is not an interest-only mortgage) and when your home appreciates in value. Most homes will increase in value over time. However, over short and occasionally long periods of time, homes, like any investment, can lose value. Home ownership should be a long-term decision. *Remember that your home is an illiquid investment, meaning it can take a considerable amount of time to sell your home at a fair price to a buyer.* Consider renting if your timeframe for owning a home is less than 4 years due to the high costs of selling a home (mortgage fees, Realtor fees, closing fees, etc.).

Look Beyond The Monthly Payment

By careful to find a home you can comfortably afford. A key mistake homeowners make is to grossly underestimate the ongoing costs of homeownership, including updates, repairs, utilities, special assessments, furnishings, etc. Also remember that as your home appreciates so too does the property tax assessment. If you are in a high property tax state and home prices start to move upward in your neighborhood, expect routine increases in property taxes from your property tax assessor. I've found tax assessor offices to be one of the most efficient areas of local government when it comes to increasing property taxes! Living beneath your means is a key ingredient to long-term financial wellness. *Make sure the home you own does not become an all-consuming drain on your finances.* For long-term financial wellness you'll need to have enough resources left over to invest systematically in company sponsored retirement plans and in personal investments.

One final point to keep in mind is that your house is not a retirement asset. *It is a place to live.* Do not expect to sell your house, buy a smaller one, and use the difference to help fund your retirement. It generally won't happen. In fact, the older you get, the more you will likely want to stay in your house!

Take the time to review and complete the *Action Step Checklist* on the following page. Protecting what you have is crucial for long-term financial wellness. In **Step #7**, we'll examine the role insurance has in protecting your health, life, income and financial assets...

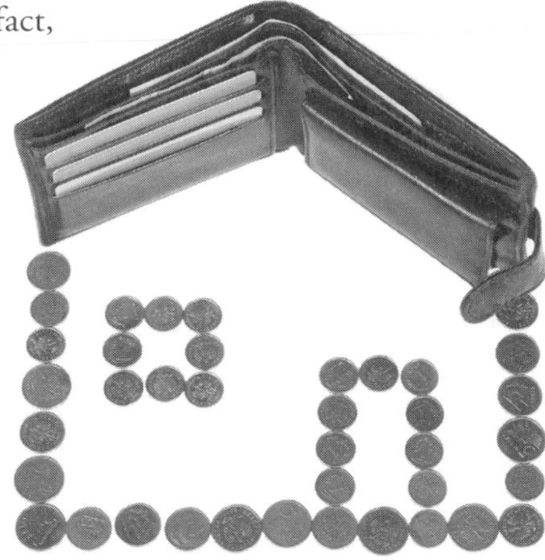

6

ACTION STEP CHECKLIST

Step #6 Action Step Checklist

Congratulations on completing Step #6. Listed are some key Action Steps to consider from this chapter. When you've finished the Action Step, place a ✓ next to the Step to document your progress.

Here is your Action Step Checklist from Step #6:

- ______When investing, remember that risk and return are inseparable. If you want a better long-term return, you must be prepared to accept more risk. Risk can be effectively managed through a diversified mix of stock and bond investments. Evaluate your current investments to ensure that you are taking the right amount of risk for your age and investment timeframe.

- ______Cash-type investments offer the lowest risk in the short-term (usually over a one to two year period) but in the longer-term offer the lowest returns, thereby increasing the risk you won't be able to achieve your financial goals. Cash-type investments are essential for building your short-term emergency fund. Your short-term emergency fund should provide from three to six months' of anticipated living expenses.

- ______Remember that mutual funds and exchange-traded funds offer instant diversification and are often the best option for securing long-term investment growth.

- ______If adding bonds to your portfolio, a good strategy for most people is to purchase a bond mutual fund. Remember to carefully read the bond fund's prospectus before investing. However, U.S. Savings Bonds can offer an excellent value for long-term savings and can be purchased direct from the U.S. Treasury. Some employers also offer payroll deduction for U.S. Savings Bond investments.

- ______Dividend reinvestment plans (DRIPS) offer a convenient and low cost way for individual investors to purchase individual company shares.

- ______When choosing any mutual fund look at long-term returns (over a period of several years) and also look at fund management fees. Pay particular attention to the fund's annual fees and whether a front-end load is charged. Choose funds with the best combination of returns and reasonable overall fees.

- ______Rebalance your investment portfolio once each year to ensure that you continue to have the right mix of stock and bond investments over time.

- ______Owning a home is a great investment for most people. Be careful with other direct investments in real estate due to cost and complexity. Real Estate Investment Trusts offer investors a method to invest in real estate utilizing professional management.

Spending Pl
March 2007
Introduction
Eligibility and Enrollment
Who Is Eligible
How to Enroll
When Participation Begins
Open Enrollment Period
How the Plan Works
Health Care Premium
Making Salary Redi
Expense Reimburs
7
Optional Life
Ages < 25
25 - 29
30 - 34
35 - 39
40 - 44
45 - 49
50 - 54
55 - 59
60 - 64
65 - 69
70 - 74
75 & >
Dependent Life
Spouse
$10,000
$25,000
$50,000
$75,000
$100,000
Benefits

STEP 7
Insurance—Protecting What You Have

"The best time to purchase insurance is when you don't need it!"

Insurance Is Protection

When you think of insurance, think protection. Insurance is designed to protect you from unexpected events that can cause you financial distress. In this chapter, I will review key insurance options for your consideration. Having adequate insurance is essential for building long-term financial wellness. Without ample insurance, you are placing at serious risk the financial assets you've accumulated if the unexpected occurs such as a major disability, accidental injury, major illness or premature death.

Being over or under-insured is a challenge we all face. Being over-insured results in having duplicate coverage or too much coverage for an unexpected event. When you are over-insured, you are essentially wasting money for coverage you don't need. Fortunately, this isn't a problem for most people. Instead, the bigger risk is being under-insured or having no insurance coverage at all for insurable risks that can cause you serious financial hardship. Insurance functions well when it is used for protection. Some insurance products take on investment characteristics like cash value life insurance products and annuities. Whenever an insurance product crosses the line from protection to investment, *be very careful*. High fees and costly surrender charges make cash value life insurance and deferred annuities poor investments for most people.

Insurance Through Your Employer

Most employers will include in your benefits package a variety of insurance that is either provided to you (once you meet eligibility requirements) or is available to you on a voluntary basis. Voluntary insurance offerings usually require you to choose and pay on your own for the insurance option that you deem necessary. Following is a list of insurance offerings that may be available through your employer:

- **Health Insurance**—this is the most important form of employer-sponsored insurance coverage. Why? Because just one unexpected accident or hospitalization can easily run $10,000 dollars or more. Most people simply don't have that much cash immediately available to cover large hospital and related physician expenses. Furthermore, purchasing health insurance on your own can be very expensive, and it can be difficult to secure comprehensive coverage from an insurer, especially if you have chronic health conditions like diabetes or a history of heart disease. If you need to find health insurance on your own, a good website to visit is eHealthInsurance.com (www.ehealthinsurance.com). If you need to find a qualified health insurance agent in your area, The National Association of Health Insurance Underwriters website (www.nahu.org) can help you find one. Unless you are health insurance-savvy, you'll need to seek the assistance of a qualified health insurance agent—health insurance policies and products are very complex.

  If your spouse has good health plan coverage through an employer, you may decide to "opt-out" of your own employer's coverage. It usually makes sound financial sense to have just one health insurance policy, especially if the policy covers comprehensive medical procedures and services. Some people fear that, if they turn down their employer's health insurance benefit, they won't have coverage if their spouses later lose their coverage. This is an unfounded fear for most people.

  Under the *Health Insurance Portability and Accountability Act of 1996* (HIPAA), the employee or dependent must request special enrollment within 30 days of the loss of health insurance coverage to be offered health insurance by the employer-sponsored plan.[1] When this notice is provided by the employee or dependent, the employer and health insurer must offer you and your dependents continued health coverage under the "special enrollment" provisions of HIPAA. A qualifying event includes the loss of a job or insurance coverage by a spouse or dependent. Be sure to check with your employer before declining health insurance coverage to ensure that your employer is aware of this "special enrollment" provision of HIPAA.

- **Life Insurance**—most employers will provide some form of life insurance for you in the event of death, and some may even extend a small amount of coverage to your dependents. Although this is a good benefit, rarely is the amount of employer-provided coverage enough insurance. Find out if your employer offers additional coverage for an added charge. This can be a good way to buy additional insurance coverage at group rates, especially if the cost is less than the cost of similar policies offered on the Internet or by your life insurance agent. Also, buying additional coverage from your employer is especially attractive if you are in poor health or if you have ever been turned down for insurance. The reason is that individual employees' health usually is ignored when insurance companies set group premiums. Should you choose to purchase additional life insurance through your employer, find out if it is "portable," meaning you can take it with you should you leave employment.

- **Dental and Vision Insurance**—your employer may provide these benefits as part of your benefits package without extra charge once you meet eligibility requirements. Other employers make these benefits optional, meaning you pay for coverage if you choose to have it. Generally dental coverage makes good sense, especially if you have children. The need for vision coverage depends on the need you and your dependents have for vision services, including eye examinations and the cost for prescription lenses and frames.

- **Disability Insurance**—many employers will offer disability insurance as a fringe benefit once you meet eligibility requirements. *If you don't have disability insurance available through your employer, consider obtaining it.* The probability that you'll have a disability keeping you away from work more than 30 days is quite high over the course of a career. Consider these facts regarding disability:

> **"Nearly 33 percent of all people will suffer a serious disability between the ages of 35 and 65. The average disability will last more than five years, but for 30 percent of those disabled, it will persist for life."[2]**

These are certainly sobering statistics. Unfortunately your bills don't stop accumulating should you become disabled. In fact, they may increase. That's why some people call disability *living death*—income ends, the same as if the person with the disability has died, but living expenses continue. As a result, disability coverage is an essential element to protecting your income throughout your working years. *If you are single, after securing health insurance, this is the most important insurance coverage you can have.* Without a spouse to provide ongoing financial support due to disability, singles can face a financial crisis if income is lost for a significant period of time. Typically long-term disability insurance will cover a maximum of two-thirds of your current income, and many policies cover only 50% or 60%. Total income replacement coverage is not available due to cost and due to the need to provide an incentive for people to go back to work following recovery from disability.

Know Your Benefit Options

Remember to take the time to know the benefits your employer offers. With employer-sponsored benefit plans changing at a rapid pace, make sure you attend all employer-sponsored benefit meetings, and know all the benefit options available to you. With employers offering an increasing number of benefit choices, it's now more important than ever for you to know your available insurance options.

If your employer's benefits program does not include the insurance options described above, you may need to seek coverage on your own or through your spouse, especially for health insurance. For most people, the risk of a serious accident or illness and its associated cost is simply too much to absorb without some type of health insurance. If you do not have health insurance, seek the assistance of a qualified health insurance agent to find coverage you can afford. One large healthcare bill can wipe out years of savings. *In fact, the inability to pay large healthcare bills is the number one reason for personal bankruptcies in the U.S.*[3]

Insurance Coverage For Personal Protection

Employer-sponsored insurance benefits can provide you with a solid foundation to protect you from a variety of unexpected losses. However, there are other types of insurance you must have in place outside of any coverage you gain through your employer.

For most people, a good start for finding personal insurance to adequately cover your risk of significant loss is to find a competent insurance agent to advise you on appropriate coverage. *A good agent is absolutely invaluable for most people.* Insurance can be extremely complicated, especially when it comes to determining which provisions you do and do not need. A close friend of mine grew up in the insurance business, succeeding his father in the family insurance agency. One day we were discussing the new Medicare Part D Prescription Drug Act benefits, and I mentioned some of the "exclusions" with this coverage. After I completed my explanation of known exclusions, he said with a smile on his face:

> **"In the insurance business, my father taught me at a young age that the policy's large print giveith and the small print takeith away!"[4]**

How true this is!

In this section, I will review some of the major forms of personal insurance that you should consider to preserve your assets from unexpected losses. Depending on your personal situation and the coverage you may have in place from an employer, you may have adequate coverage. But make sure you discuss all coverages you have with a respected insurance agent. A good agent will provide you with sound advice regarding the adequacy of current policies and identify gaps in coverage that may cause problems.

Life Insurance: Term Or Cash Value?

All life insurance policies can be categorized broadly as either term or permanent (also known as cash value) insurance. Term insurance provides temporary coverage for periods ranging from 1 year to perhaps as long as 30 years. When coverage is needed for longer periods of time, such as until one's death, permanent life insurance is more appropriate.

So which type is best for you? The answer depends on the reasons why you need coverage. If you are trying to protect your young children, term insurance with a maturity matching the time they will be your dependents is most appropriate. If your goal is to provide your spouse with protection until you retire at age 65, term is again appropriate. *But if your goal is to provide your estate, heirs, charities, your church, or your business with cash at your death, term insurance is totally inappropriate.* You may not die until you are in your 70s, 80s, 90s, or even later. Term insurance either won't be available at those ages, or the cost will make it prohibitively expensive.

There is another consideration: cost. Permanent insurance costs between 5 and 20 times as much as the same amount of term insurance. Most people between the ages of 20 and perhaps as old as 50 find the cost of permanent life insurance to be an extravagance and many don't have the money to buy adequate coverage. As a result, the use of term insurance dominates permanent insurance in this age group. On the other hand, older wealthy people can afford adequate amounts of permanent insurance and often have estate and business needs requiring permanent insurance. If you are so lucky to be in this situation, buy permanent life insurance, not term.

How Much Life Insurance Do You Need?

If you are single and have no dependents, your answer may very well be **zero**. If you're single and have accumulated enough assets to cover your debts and funeral expenses, you probably don't need life insurance, unless you plan to leave something to a relative, friend or charitable organization. So how much does a funeral cost? According to the American Association of Retired Persons (AARP), the average cost for an adult funeral ranges from $4,500 to $5,500. About one-third of that is for the cost of the casket alone. An in-ground burial can add another $2,400 to the total.[5]

For those with dependents, the amount of life insurance needed becomes a more complicated task. There is no general agreement amongst veteran life insurance agents regarding how much life insurance you'll need. Figuring out how much is needed is as much an art as a science. **Appendix 7-1** (located in the Appendix Section in the back of the book) provides an excellent way for you to estimate the amount of life insurance you will need. Take the time to complete this handy *Life Insurance Needs Checklist* to make sure that you have adequate life insurance coverage.

If you use your favorite Internet search engine to search for "Life insurance needed calculator," you will find thousands of sites to help you determine the amount of life insurance you'll need. Get estimates from at least five sites; ignore estimates that are obviously too high or too low, and average those that remain. This is a great way to figure out how much coverage you'll need.

The Cost Of Term Life Insurance

The good news for those who need life insurance is that term life insurance coverage is relatively inexpensive for individuals in reasonably good health and under the age of 55. For example, the cost of a $750,000, 20-year level premium term life insurance policy for a non-smoking male, age 47, is about $100 per month.[6] That's considerable insurance coverage for a relatively low monthly payment. The website I consulted provided me with a listing of several carriers that would provide me with a level premium term policy for 20 years. All of the illustrative rates are of course contingent on passing a physical exam and completing a detailed health questionnaire by the insurance carrier. There are a number of good online sources you can use to find a carrier that makes the most sense for you. A site I recommend for term life insurance quotes is www.insure.com. This site provides quotes from 40 companies without notifying insurers of your inquiry. This allows you to get several quotes from reputable insurers and to purchase a policy (subject to medical underwriting and a physical exam) online.

Whenever possible, I believe you should use a qualified life insurance agent to help you select the best term insurance possible. But a little homework on your part prior to your meeting with a life insurance agent makes sense

(be sure to perform the life insurance estimate in Appendix 7-1 before meeting with an agent). When purchasing life insurance, you'll get the most flexibility from a life insurance agent who represents multiple life insurance carriers, but even captive agents who represent just one company may be able to provide competitive rates for term coverage. For life insurance purchases, stick with life insurance carriers that have at least an "A" rating from A.M. Best, an independent insurance rating service. A.M. Best has been in the insurance rating business since the early 1900s and is a recognized leader in providing unbiased, independent ratings covering the financial health of life insurance companies (but not the quality of policies).[7] Insure.com and other Internet sites give you the A.M. Best ratings for each company offering you a quote.

Advice On Deferred Payment And Immediate Payment Annuities

Annuities are contracts offered by life insurance companies that pay a certain amount of money each month for a specified time period to the contract owner (the annuitant). Annuitants fund these contracts either by making a lump-sum payment to the insurer or by making a series of monthly payments to the insurance company. Most annuities are purchased by people whose goal is to guarantee monthly income during their retirement years.

Annuities funded by a series of monthly payments over many years are called "deferred annuities," because the annuitant usually "defers" the withdrawal period until retirement. A lump-sum payment also can be used to fund a deferred annuity. But when a person makes a lump-sum payment and immediately begins monthly withdrawals, the annuity is called an "immediate" annuity. Almost always, immediate annuities are used to provide income to a retiring employee.

Deferred payment and immediate payment annuities come in two basic forms: *fixed and variable*. The fixed payment deferred annuity usually provides a fixed interest rate—which may or may not adjust to match changes over time in market rates of interest—for a specified period of time. With the fixed payment immediate annuity, the annuity contract holder receives a fixed sum of money typically each month for life. The biggest drawback to this type of annuity is that, unless an expensive inflation adjustment rider is purchased, inflation will erode the purchasing power of the annuity over a period of years.

The second type of annuity is a variable payment annuity. This annuity allows you to select investments (typically stock and bond funds similar to mutual funds but formally called *separate accounts* or *sub-accounts*) in your annuity account. If your investments do well, your annuity payment will rise. If your investments do poorly, your annuity payment will be smaller than projected.

A popular hybrid annuity, the equity indexed annuity, combines elements of the fixed payment annuity and the variable payment annuity into one product. Beware of this product, however. Most equity indexed annuities are laced with fees, high annual expenses, backend commissions that don't end for many years, and so called "caps," limiting the upside growth of your investment portfolio. The fine print generally allows the annuity issuer to change the "cap" rules during the contract (effectively lowering the possible investment return), making this type of annuity suspect for most investors. In addition, equity indexed annuities have a bad reputation brought about by their all-too-common and inappropriate sales to the elderly. As a result, many reputable financial services firms have banned their agents from selling them.

Deferred Payment Annuities—Proceed With Caution

Understand one very important point whenever you get a deferred payment annuity pitch from a financial professional: *The compensation he or she receives is often very lucrative!* Hence, the enthusiasm for some misguided agents to sell a deferred payment annuity product with gusto to those who can buy it. I'm not saying that you should avoid purchasing a deferred annuity, especially if you earn a very high income and you've maxed out the contributions to retirement accounts. What I am saying is buyer beware whenever someone contacts you to discuss the latest and greatest deferred annuity product. *Unless you have exhausted all of your 401(k) options at work and you've fully funded your IRA for the year, you probably should not consider a deferred annuity product. It's pretty much that simple.* You get similar tax-deferral benefits with the funding of 401(k)s and IRAs, generally with a lot less in fees paid out in commissions to the agent, lower annual fees for administration and no insurance risk charges.

Immediate Fixed Payment Annuities—An Excellent Retirement Funding Option

Immediate payment fixed annuities are usually purchased by people at retirement, when lump-sum distributions are received from pension plans. In exchange for one lump-sum payment, the annuity issuer will make ongoing payments (typically monthly) to you, the annuitant, for life or a shorter period of time (your choice). A life annuity will have a smaller monthly payment than an annuity which pays benefits for a shorter time period such as 10 or 20 years. *One huge advantage of an immediate payment life annuity is that you will never outlive your annuity payments.* One of the biggest risks retirees face is that they will run out of money before they run out of time here on Earth!

You should never use all of your retirement nest egg to purchase one or more immediate payment annuities. The percentage of your retirement portfolio that should be considered for an immediate payment fixed annuity will vary for each individual. Your current overall health status should be a major factor in selecting an immediate annuity. If you have poor health, an immediate annuity will likely not be a good choice. With most immediate annuities, you are betting you will live longer than projections made by the insurance company.

The balance of your retirement portfolio not devoted to an immediate payment annuity should be invested in a broadly diversified, conservative mix of equities, bonds and short-term savings investments. By doing this, you'll give yourself vital inflation protection and enhance the prospect for prudent growth in your retirement portfolio. In most cases, you should limit the investment in immediate payment annuities to no more than 50% of your retirement assets. A website I recommend for finding payouts you will receive from different annuities can be found at Immediate Annuities.com (www.immediateannuities.com). This site will provide annuity payouts from a number of highly-rated annuity providers and will give you an excellent idea on the size of monthly expected payouts from an immediate annuity purchase.

Annuities are complex. Most people are well-served to make a decision to purchase an annuity with the advice of a competent financial professional. The decision to buy an annuity will have long-term consequences. Once you begin receiving annuity payments, you are bound by the annuity contract's terms for its life. As a result, you must take the time to know what you are buying.

Annuity payments are not guaranteed by the federal government or by the state government in the state where you live. This means that when purchasing an immediate payment annuity, it is vitally important to check the financial rating of the annuity insurer. Financial ratings are important, because if your annuity insurer encounters financial difficulties, your ability to collect promised annuity payments could be compromised. Stick with annuity insurers that have an investment rating of excellent (usually an A rating or better) from A.M. Best.

Long-Term Care Insurance—Think Of It As Asset Protection

Long-term care insurance might be about the last type of insurance you think about during your career. **My advice:** *think again.* If you plan to retire with total investments, including the value of your home, of at least $200,000, you should consider the purchase of long-term care insurance. A lot of people think that long-term care insurance is part of Medicare. It's not. Private health insurance also does not pay for long-term care, often referred to as "custodial care." Nor is long-term care just for the elderly. Approximately 40% of people needing long-term care in the United States are between the ages of 18 and 64.[8]

So how much does a full year of long-term care cost for home healthcare or nursing home care? According to a MetLife Market Survey on nursing home and home healthcare costs conducted in 2006, the average cost of a private room in a nursing home was $75,190 per year! Costs vary considerably by state and by the type of services selected. However, with the number of aging "baby boomers" on the rise, demand for long-term care services will strain the limited supply of long-term care resources, resulting in rising costs for these essential services.

The best time to buy any type of insurance is when you don't need it. This especially holds true for long-term care. If you try buying it in your 60s or 70s, your health may be such that you will be considered "uninsurable" by long-term care insurance carriers, or the premium might be relatively high. That's why I recommend people consider purchasing long-term care during the later stages of their working careers, typically beginning around 50 years of age. Like life insurance, premiums are lower the younger you begin coverage and your probability for getting insured will likely be higher at a younger age.

Don't try to purchase a long-term care policy on your own. Consult with a specialist in long-term care before buying a policy. Get quotes from at least 3 long-term care insurers, and make sure your agent compares quotes that include similar benefits. Long-term care policies are created differently, and there are a lot of choices to make when purchasing a policy. There are 650,000 combinations of coverages from a bare-bones policy. Include the various payment options (quarterly, monthly, etc.), and the number of combinations exceeds 8 million. Do you see why you might need the advice and help from a long-term care insurance agent?

Consider This:

Remember the late movie actor, Christopher Reeve? At the age of 43, he suffered a freak accident riding a horse and was permanently disabled for many years until his death. Reeve spent years receiving custodial care before his death.

Here are essential items to have in your policy:

Inflation rider—You definitely want this with any policy you purchase. Why? Because if you need long-term care services, you'll more than likely need them many years after you purchase your long-term care policy, resulting in much higher prices for similar services in today's dollars. Typical annual inflation adjustments are 5% simple interest and 5% compounded interest. Choose the 5% compound option, because long-term care costs will more than likely increase by at least this amount per year.

Elimination period—The elimination period is the amount of time from the start of receiving long-term care services to the time your policy starts paying for services. Choose a policy that only has one elimination period for the life of the policy. Typical elimination periods are from 30 to 90 days. Most people choose a 90 day elimination period to keep premiums lower. Most people should be able to afford the first 90 days of long-term care.

Insurance company rating—Stick with insurance companies that carry at least an "A" rating by the major insurance rating services. You want to make sure that the insurer you select will be in business should you need payment for long-term care services.

Purchase with your spouse—If you are married, you and your spouse will receive a discount if both spouses purchase coverage from the same insurance carrier. Why? Insurers know that when there is a spouse there is a built in caregiver who will often perform many of the custodial care services that a home healthcare provider or a nursing home would provide. This serves to delay or even eliminate the need to access long-term care benefits, resulting in savings to the insurance carrier. A portion of anticipated savings are reflected in the lower policy premium when both spouses have long-term care coverage from the same insurance carrier.

Level of care—There are a number of ways to receive long-term care services. Make sure your policy covers all levels of care including skilled or non-skilled care, delivered in any setting including the home, in an assisted living center, in an adult day care center or in a nursing home.

Benefit Period and Benefit Max—Spend some time (or have your agent) research the cost of long-term care services in your community. If you need full-time nursing home care, your costs will likely range from $150 to $300 per day. Standard benefit periods of coverage will be from 3 to 5 years. A lifetime benefit is available from some insurers, and the extra premium is about 35% more than the 5 year benefit period. Since people are living longer, it makes sense to buy a policy with a benefit period as long as possible (remember to include the inflation rider). Spend most of your time working on this area of your policy because it's essential that you have the right amount of coverage in place when you need it.[9]

Employers are beginning to look at long-term care as a workplace benefit, especially as the U.S. workforce ages. Find out if your employer offers long-term care coverage. If so, take a good look at choosing this benefit, because group rates are often lower than rates for individually purchased policies. Since long-term care policies are "portable," you'll be able to take your policy with you when you leave employment. Don't leave long-term care coverage to chance. Carefully consider long-term care as an asset preservation strategy and as much needed coverage if you should you need long-term care during your lifetime.

Personal Property Insurance

Most people have a need to insure their homes. Even if you are a renter, you'll want to look at renters insurance. Even people with modest personal belongings are often surprised to discover they have accumulated significant personal property and could incur a severe financial hardship in the event of a fire, hurricane, tornado, theft or other unexpected event.

One way to save significantly on personal insurance needs is to place all or most of your policies with one insurance carrier. Insurance carriers will usually provide a multi-policy discount as an incentive to keep policyholders from purchasing coverages elsewhere. This reduces the turnover of policyholders and results in greater policy retention for insurers. The lower cost associated with reduced retention expenses is passed along to multi-line policyholders in lower premiums. Savings from buying all of your coverages from the same insurance company can be substantial, often 5-15% on each type of policy.

I've taken advantage of my insurer's multi-line discount for a number of years and have enjoyed significant savings. In the review that follows, I will reference some items to keep in mind when insuring your property and your vehicle. Although there are other types of personal property and casualty (lawsuit) coverage you might need, getting the proper coverage for your property and vehicle represents the foundation of adequate property and casualty coverage.

Property Insurance Suggestions

The first step to take before seeking personal property protection is to make a written or video inventory of the significant items you own. Here are some suggestions to help you prepare your inventory:

- **Prepare an inventory for each room of your home, condo or apartment**—label each room with its contents. This will help you to organize and update your inventory. Make sure that you keep the recorded inventory in a safe location away from your dwelling. Consider the use of a safe deposit box or a file at work.

- **Make a videotape or take pictures of special value items**—keep these items offsite with your written property inventory so that they can be quickly retrieved in the event of a loss. The more documentation you have regarding lost assets, the easier it will be to reach a fair and equitable settlement with your insurance carrier.

- **Add up the approximate value of what you own from your inventory sheet**—this will provide you with a general idea of how much insurance to purchase for coverage of your valuable contents. Understand that you'll also need to cover "incidental" items in the event of a total loss. So, it's generally a good idea to add another 20 percent to the value you calculate. Most insurers cover loss to contents up to 50% to 75% (depending on the insurer) of the coverage you carry on the dwelling. If there is a loss, you'll have to prove you actually owned the lost personal property. That's the purpose of the household inventory.

- **Keep sales receipts of significant purchases with your recorded inventory**—this will help you to substantiate the value of any lost property.

- **Consider the purchase of special endorsements to cover rare items**—insurance policies don't cover everything, especially if you have quite a bit of jewelry, collectibles, artwork, firearms, or other valuables that exceed the limits of your policy. Insurance carriers have endorsements that cover these special, identified items for a modest, extra fee. It most often makes sense to spend extra for the endorsement to cover special items.

You should work with a qualified property and casualty agent when choosing property insurance. One way to save significantly on your premium is to increase your deductible. For homeowners, increasing your deductible from $250 to $1,000 can lower your premium by at least ten percent. Also make sure your property insurance has either replacement cost or inflation coverage on both the dwelling and its contents. Insurance carriers are moving away from full replacement cost coverage. However, you should be able to find coverage reflecting the increased cost to rebuild a home or to replace the contents in your home or apartment.

Vehicle Insurance

Your age, marital status, driving record, credit score, type of vehicle and where you live are key determinants of your auto insurance rates. Those with years of accident-free driving and no traffic violations will save considerably on insurance. That's why most of us pay a different rate for vehicle insurance. There are a host of factors that determine your final rate. In addition, every auto insurance carrier applies differing underwriting standards to determine the risks they wish to insure. By shopping around, you can often save considerably on auto insurance.

Most people are best served when working with a qualified agent due to the complexity of auto insurance. If you are insurance-savvy, consider quotes from "direct-to-consumer" insurance companies like Geico, Progressive or AIG Direct. You might save premium dollars by going the direct route. Many people have saved money by purchasing insurance directly from the insurer. A good website to visit for online vehicle insurance is offered by InsWeb (www.insweb.com). Regardless of how you purchase your insurance (direct or through an agent), here are some points to consider:

- **Increase your collision deductible**—get quotes on differing deductible levels. By doing this, you'll find premium savings up to 40%.[10]

- **List safety features and anti-theft devices**—insurers will usually give discounts for extra air bags and anti-theft devices. Find out which added features your insurer will discount and make sure you report them to your agent or insurer.

- **Drop collision coverage if your vehicle is worth less than $1,000**—you can save a bundle when you drop collision coverage. If you purchase collision coverage when your vehicle is worth less than $1,000, you will likely pay too much for this form of protection. You are usually better off pocketing the collision savings in exchange for lower insurance rates.

- **If you have teen drivers, seek discounts**—you'll experience true insurance "sticker shock" when you add a teen to your coverage. But there are things you can do to lower the added insurance expense. One way is to add the teen to the lowest value vehicle only if this is the vehicle that the teen will be primarily driving. Also find out if your insurance carrier offers a "good student" discount. My insurance carrier discounts my teen son's insurance by 10% based on his completion of a driving program, remaining traffic and accident ticket-free and the ongoing maintenance of at least a "B" average in high school.

When purchasing any type of insurance, you'll want to make sure that you have the best coverage possible for the premium paid. The more risk you are willing to assume, primarily through increased deductibles, the more you will save on insurance. Determine how much financial risk you can take and set your deductible accordingly, balancing the ongoing premium savings with the added risk you are assuming with the higher deductible. *Ultimately you want to know what you are buying, because surprises in insurance are rarely pleasant.*

Personal Liability Umbrella Coverage

We live in a lawsuit-intensive society, and if you are ever a defendant in a personal liability lawsuit involving an automobile accident or an accident on your property, hang on to your wallet! Judgments against you can involve staggering sums of money. Personal liability umbrella protection can provide peace of mind from the potential devastation of a six or seven figure lawsuit for liability that is your fault or the fault of one of your dependents—think teen driver!

A personal liability umbrella policy pays for expenses above the stated policy limits of your homeowners, renters and auto policies. It even covers you for lawsuits involving libel and slander. When you look at your liability coverage for the auto and homeowners policies you have in force, coverage often does not exceed $300,000. With an umbrella policy, covered liability expenses that exceed your individual policy limits are paid by your umbrella policy. These policies are issued in increments of one million dollars and will cost anywhere from $150 to $300 per year for the first million of coverage and just $75 for the next million in coverage.[11] I call it cheap coverage for a very real threat to your financial well-being. *Bottom line:* Get umbrella coverage to protect your current assets and your greatest asset, your lifetime earnings.

Some personal liability lawsuit judgments attach claims to your future earnings (called garnishments) if you do not have sufficient assets to pay the judgment amount. So whatever stage of life you are in, strongly consider the purchase of umbrella liability coverage. Remember to consult with a qualified insurance agent to ensure that your underlying insurance policies have sufficient liability coverage to qualify for umbrella liability coverage.

In this chapter, I've highlighted major insurance coverages you should have to protect your health, your income, your life, your retirement, your property and your vehicle. Having the proper level of insurance is a foundation for building sustainable, long-term financial wellness.

Take the time to review and complete the *Action Step Checklist* on the following page. In **Step #8**, we'll review planning for long-term goals and the steps you can take to realize the long-term goals you've established…

7
ACTION STEP CHECKLIST

Step #7 Action Step Checklist

Congratulations on completing Step #7. Listed are some key Action Steps to consider from this chapter. When you've finished the Action Step, place a ✓ next to the Step to document your progress.

Here is your Action Step Checklist from Step #7:

- ____ Insurance should be purchased for protection. If you own a permanent life insurance policy, take a careful look at it. It might make sense for you to keep the policy in force. However, you might be better served with term insurance if you are in relatively good health. Most people are best served by sticking with term life insurance.

- ____ Consider disability insurance to protect your greatest asset—your ability to earn a future income. Many employers offer adequate disability coverage. If you do not have coverage through your employer, consider purchasing a disability policy on your own.

- ____ Get a solid estimate of how much life insurance you need by completing the Life Insurance Needs Estimate in Appendix 7-1.

- ____ If you are close to retirement and are in good health, consider the purchase of an immediate payment life annuity. With this type of annuity, you receive an income payment for life. Be sure to choose an annuity that is issued by an insurer that has an excellent credit rating from a major rating service like A.M. Best. Never devote more than 50% of your retirement assets to an annuity purchase unless an expensive inflation adjustment rider is purchased. Because annuities are complex, seek the advice of a competent financial professional before purchasing any annuity product.

- ____ If you are over the age of 50, consider purchasing a long-term care insurance policy. As people live longer, the probability of needing long-term care services later in life increases. The average cost of full time assisted care services can exceed $75,000 per year.

- ____ Make sure that you have adequate coverage on your personal property and vehicles. Take a look at deductibles on all policies. You might find that it makes sense to increase your deductibles to reduce your premiums.

- ____ Check out the cost of a personal liability umbrella policy to cover you for personal liability judgments that exceed the liability limits on your property and vehicles. Amounts of umbrella coverage are usually sold in increments of one million dollars. For many people, the annual cost will be less than $300 per million of coverage.

STEP 8
Planning For Long-Term Goals

"The plans you make today will impact your future and your overall financial wellness."

What Are Your Long-Term Goals?

When you think of a long-term goal think 5 years or longer in the future. Your long-term goals will change during your lifetime. If you are early in your career, a long-term goal may involve paying off all higher education debt in 5 to 7 years, or it may involve saving enough for a down payment on a house within 6 years. Conversely, in the twilight of your career, you may be focused on paying off all forms of debt and accumulating enough assets for a secure retirement. The "long-term" is here before you know it. Procrastination is your biggest hurdle to overcome when it comes to identifying your long-term goals. Here are 3 steps you can take to establish meaningful short and long-term goals.

1. **Goal Planning.** Write down goals that you have for yourself in the future. This is where you let your mind wander, because each person will have unique goals and will define each goal differently. After listing each goal, provide a date in the future when you'd like the goal to become a reality. You'll find that some of the listed goals will have a timeframe of less than 5 years. Any goal with a timeframe of less than 5 years should be considered a short-term goal. Also understand that not all goals can be measured financially. For instance, you should set personal short and long-term goals. Short-term personal goals may involve starting a consistent exercise program that results in a loss of 15 pounds with lowered blood pressure and cholesterol levels. A short-term financial goal may involve paying off all credit card balances within the

next three years. A helpful way to plan meaningful goals is to put your goals into categories and within each category list whether the goal is short-term (less than 5 years on the horizon) or long-term (5 or more years).

Here are four suggested categories for your goals:

- **Personal Development Goals**—these goals relate to your personal development and can include improving existing relationships with family members, coworkers, enhancing skills in a targeted area, finishing a degree, starting or maintaining a personal fitness program, etc. Complete **Appendix 8-1** (located in the Appendix Section in the back of the book) to highlight your personal goals.

- **Career Goals**—where do you see yourself in your current career in the next one, five or ten years? One thing for sure is that the workplace is changing rapidly. By focusing on where you want to go with your career, you'll examine the steps you'll need to take to move your career forward to reach your desired goal. Few career opportunities "just happen." They usually come to those who have prepared themselves for the next step in their career. How do your skills stack up? Chances are you'll need to commit to ongoing career development to keep your skills relevant in today's rapidly changing workplace. If you strive for a different position or a different career path, find out the types of skills you'll need to get there. Skill development takes time and effort. Find out if your employer offers additional training opportunities that will help you realize your career goals. If not, find out how you can get the necessary skills to help you reach your goals. **Appendix 8-2** is provided to list career goals that are important to you.

- **Financial Goals**—what do you want your finances to look like in one, three, five and ten year increments? Focus on your current non-mortgage debt. Establish goals for paying off all credit card balances within a defined period of time (hopefully within 5 years). Take a look at education for yourself, children or grandchildren. How much do you want to have saved to fund education? How much do you want to contribute each year to retirement accounts? How about large purchases for items such as vehicles or the purchase of a home? Refer to **Appendix 8-3** to list your financial goals.

- **Spiritual or Higher Purpose Goals**—I'm not attempting to preach any particular religion here. But the fact is that most people believe in God. And as such most people believe that there is something that will last well beyond our time here on Earth as we know it. Even if you are atheist in your belief system, I believe it is important for your overall sense of well-being to somehow reach out and make life better for others. Think about organizations or "causes" that are important to you and get involved with them through your time and even through your financial resources. Giving of both our time and our finances to churches, missions, charities or other valuable social causes truly adds a special dimension to our lives. **Appendix 8-4** allows you to record your spiritual or higher purpose goals in life.

Take the time to determine what is important in your "journey" through this life and support those organizations and causes that give life a special meaning. Take the time to develop your faith or belief system. It will help you to understand yourself better and to develop a purpose during your very limited time on this Earth. It will also help you to understand others better and provide you with a solid foundation for overall "wellness" throughout your life.

2. **Goal Monitoring.** After identifying the goals that are important to you, it is important to put into motion a plan of action to attain each goal. Some goals will lose significance as life events change and new goals will emerge. However, certain goals should remain consistent over several years. That's why it's important to periodically monitor your progress on goal setting to determine if your timeframe for goal attainment is on track or whether adjustments will need to be made.

3. **Goal Attainment.** This is the desired result of the planning you've done in Step #1. The attainment of goals can be incredibly rewarding. Lifelong goal setting is an essential process in developing overall wellness and is critical for the development of long-term financial wellness.

In this chapter, I'll focus on key financial goals that will help you to attain financial wellness and will review methods to help you reach those goals.

Compound Interest—Unlock the 8th Wonder of the World!

To attain long-term financial goals, you need to understand and take advantage of the awesome power of compound interest. Compound interest can turn modest sums of money into extraordinary amounts after several years of accumulation. **Exhibit 8-1** illustrates how compound interest can grow investments over long periods of time. This exhibit shows how two investors, the same age, took two entirely different paths to accumulate about the same amount of money at age 65.

The Tale of Two Investors

The two individuals featured in **Exhibit 8-1** of compound interest growth (Jack and Jill) have an extra $2,000 a year to either spend or invest. Jill decides to invest the entire $2,000 right away and does so every year for six years. After six years, Jill decides to pursue other financial goals and stops investing in the account, but leaves the accumulated amount in the account to grow until the age of 65, at an annual compound rate of 12%. Jack, on the other hand, has other priorities and decides to spend the $2,000 on vacations and the latest clothing fashions. But after six years of spending the entire annual amount of $2,000, Jack decides to invest $2,000 every year until the age of 65. Jack also earns the same annual compound interest rate of 12% as Jill. At age 65, they've both accumulated about the same amount of money for their retirement years. Jill's total outlay was just $12,000, but Jack's was $2,000 per year for 37 years adding up to $74,000! Yet their nest egg at age 65 is about the same!

Jill's disciplined early savings habits and the extra time compound interest could work in her favor made her investment strategy as effective as Jack's with considerably less of an ongoing investment. This example illustrates how Jill put to work the awesome accumulating power of compound interest! Compound interest working in an investment strategy is truly the 8th wonder of the world!

To attain financial wellness, you must take advantage of compound interest by selecting the mix of investments that deliver acceptable annual returns over a period of years. Compound interest allows your investments to grow to impressive levels over a period of years. Think of compound interest as powerful fertilizer that will allow your financial garden to accumulate a bountiful yield of multiplied dollars that will secure your financial wellness for a lifetime.

Exhibit 8-1—The Power of Compound Interest Over Time[1] (Assumed Compounding Rate 12%)

Age	Jill	Jack
22	$2,240	$0
23	4,509	0
24	7,050	0
25	9,896	0
26	13,083	0
27	16,653	0
28	18,652	2,240
29	20,890	4,509
30	23,397	7,050

(Table continued on next page)

(Continued)

Exhibit 8-1—The Power of Compound Interest Over Time[1] (Assumed Compounding Rate 12%)		
Age	**Jill**	**Jack**
35	41,233	25,130
40	72,667	56,993
45	128,064	113,147
50	225,692	212,598
55	397,746	386,516
60	700,965	693,879
65	$1,235,339	$1,235,557

Individual Retirement Accounts (IRAs)

If you have a retirement account like a 401(k), 403(b) or 457 plan provided by your employer, you should participate at least to the employer's match. But what about IRAs? Almost everyone should establish an IRA at some point during his or her career.

When you look at your retirement account funding options, it can get confusing regarding where you should start with your contributions. Listed below is a recommended funding order for tax-advantaged retirement accounts that most people should follow.

1. If your employer offers a retirement savings account matching contribution, contribute at least the amount necessary to take full advantage of the employer's matching contribution.

2. Once the matching contribution threshold is met, any extra proceeds should then fund an IRA to its maximum level, if possible. If you meet the income requirements for a Roth IRA, favor it over a Traditional IRA.

3. If all IRA options are fully funded (for both you and your spouse), use any additional funds to continue funding your employer-sponsored retirement plan all the way to the maximum contribution allowed by the plan.

4. If you've reached this point, you've "maxed out" both your employer-sponsored retirement plan and your IRA for the year. Additional proceeds can be used to fund other saving, investing, or charitable giving priorities.

The Two Basic IRA Options

When it comes to IRAs, there are two basic options for individuals to consider: the Traditional IRA and the Roth IRA.[2] Annual funding maximums for both types of IRAs per eligible individual are as follows:

- For tax year 2009, $5,000; those 50 or over can contribute an additional $1,000.

Note that married couples can each contribute to an IRA even if only one spouse had earned income during the tax year and that the working spouse's earned income is enough to cover IRA contributions for both spouses. So if one or both spouses have earned income of at least $10,000 in 2009, each spouse can contribute the full $5,000 contribution to his/her IRA. For those over 50, a total of $12,000 would need to be earned for each spouse to make the maximum ($6,000) IRA contribution.

Traditional IRAs—Unless you are permanently disabled or have retired from the workforce early, you're not allowed to withdraw money (without a penalty) from a Traditional IRA until you turn 59 ½. *You and your spouse can make an annual contribution to a non-deductible IRA regardless of your earned income.* This means that the amount you place into the non-deductible IRA does not receive the benefits of a federal or state income tax deduction, but your earnings grow tax-deferred until you begin taking distributions from your IRA. You must begin making IRS calculated minimum annual withdrawals from a Traditional IRA by April 1 following the year in which you reach the age of 70 ½.[3] You may be eligible to make tax-deductible contributions to a Traditional IRA if you meet certain income requirements and you were not covered under an employer's retirement plan.

Roth IRA—The Roth IRA is a popular option for many people. Why? The Roth IRA allows for the tax-free accumulation of earnings from your account. Roth IRAs also allow additional flexibility that cannot be attained with a Traditional IRA. Although you don't receive a tax deduction on amounts you place into your Roth IRA, you receive the following benefits:

- Contributions to the account can be withdrawn free of federal income tax at any time.
- Earnings are tax-free if the account is at least five years old and you are at least 59 ½ at the time of distribution.
- Unlike Traditional IRAs, there is no mandated date to begin withdrawals and account balances transfer to designated beneficiaries tax-free.

Roth IRA Income Limits For 2009

To qualify for a Roth IRA, your modified adjusted gross income is less than:

- $176,000 for married filing jointly or qualifying widow(er);
- $10,000 for married filing separately and you lived with your spouse at any time during the year *(note: this is not a typing error, it's $10,000 in this instance)*; and
- $120,000 for single, head of household, or married filing separately and you did not live with your spouse during the year.[4]

If your income falls within the modified gross income threshold established by the IRS, you should definitely favor the Roth IRA over the Traditional IRA, even in cases where the Traditional IRA is tax-deductible. The reason why I favor the Roth over all forms of the Traditional IRA is the incredible flexibility you receive with a Roth IRA. If you should need funds for education or some other long-term goal, you can pull the amounts contributed to the Roth without penalty at any age. In addition, the tax-free nature of the Roth and the fact that distributions are never required from the account, make it an excellent tax-planning vehicle.

Higher Education Or Advanced Training Is Key To Economic Success

In today's global economy, the value of advanced educational training has never been more important for securing a good job or career. Being unskilled in our economy subjects most people to lifelong employment in low-paying, high turnover jobs. These jobs typically lack essential benefits like health insurance or pension options, which places additional financial burdens on those employed in low skill jobs.

College is not for everyone and the good news is that there are plentiful opportunities in high paying technical jobs that do not require a college degree. Examples include jobs in construction trades such as electricians, plumbers and heating and air conditioning specialists. The days of the "auto mechanic" are over. They've been replaced by highly trained "automotive technicians," who rely on advanced technology and well-honed diagnostic skills to fix vehicles. These positions pay very well and with overtime, those with the highest skills can earn six-figure incomes. There are a number of excellent programs and apprenticeships that will provide the necessary training for those who do not wish to pursue a college degree. Having specialized training or advanced education is a key element to attaining financial wellness.

Education Of U.S. Adults

In the year 2000, about 84% of American adults ages 25 and over had earned a minimum of a high school diploma, and 26% had gone on to complete a bachelor's or higher education degree program.[5] It is anticipated that the U.S. will continue to see advances in higher education completion due to the shift of the U.S. economy to more highly skilled, information-based careers.

The Bureau of Labor Statistics conducts an annual Current Population Survey. This survey tracks earnings and examines factors that determine adult earning potential. Based upon data from the survey compiled from 1997-1999, the study found that adults ages 25 to 65 who worked at any point throughout the duration of the study period received average annual earnings of $35,000.[6]

However, average earnings varied in amount by level of education. High school dropouts earned $18,900; high school graduates earned $25,900; college graduates earned $45,400; and $99,300 for persons possessing a professional degree (J.D, M.D., D.V.M., or D.D.S). *Evidence from the Current Population survey analysis suggests that each consecutive higher education level a person receives is directly related to an increase in earnings.*

College Tuition Exceeds General Inflation By A Wide Margin

Annual increases in the cost of higher education continue to exceed annual increases in the Consumer Price Index (CPI) by about a 2 to 1 margin.[7] **Exhibit 8-2** shows how annual college tuition increases have outpaced general inflation (measured by increases in CPI) starting in 1958. In every period of time examined in the Exhibit, college tuition inflation has outpaced the CPI by a wide margin. The Rate Ratio result in **Exhibit 8-2** (fourth column) represents college inflation divided by general inflation to produce the appropriate Rate Ratio.

Exhibit 8-2—College Inflation and General Inflation[8]

Year	College Inflation	General Inflation	Rate Ratio
1958-1996	7.24%	4.49%	1.61
1977-1986	9.85%	6.72%	1.47
1987-1996	6.68%	3.67%	1.82
1958-2001	6.98%	4.30%	1.62
1979-2001	7.37%	3.96%	1.86
1992-2001	4.77%	2.37%	2.01
1985-2001	6.39%	3.18%	2.01
1958-2005	6.89%	4.15%	1.66
1989-2005	5.94%	2.99%	1.99

With cutbacks in state-supported funding for public colleges and the expected increased demand for higher education, expect future college costs to continue above CPI for several years. College education and higher education generally have a very good payoff when considering the increased earnings graduates generate throughout a career.

Ideas For College Education Financing

When you read the headlines about the cost of a 4 year college education, it can lead to a major case of "sticker shock." To be sure, college education is expensive; but the cost for a quality education varies significantly. With careful planning virtually anyone can attain a college degree. *Knowing your options when it comes to college selection and college financing are key ingredients in choosing a college that meets your budget and offers a quality education.*

College Costs are Rising—For the 2008-2009 academic year, The College Board reported that average annual tuition and related fee costs for four-year public and four-year private universities were $6,585 and $25,143, respectively.[9] Add in room and board for another $7,251 at public colleges and $8,108 at private colleges and the total average tab reaches $13,836 at public universities and $33,251 at private universities. That's a lot of money!

The first step in saving for a child's college education is to secure a Social Security Number for your child. With your child's Social Security number, you can establish an account for the benefit of your child and make regular contributions to tax-free (for accumulation of earnings) college savings plans. The magic of compound interest accumulation works great in these tax-advantaged plans. **Exhibit 8-3** shows how $200 invested for a newborn at 8% per month grows to over $96,000 at age 18. These plans (called 529 plans) allow contributions to grow tax-free in the account on behalf of the minor child and any earnings are usually tax-free when used to finance qualified college or trade school expenses.

Exhibit 8-3—Growth Of Investment Saving $200 Per Month To The Age Of 18
The Power of Compounding

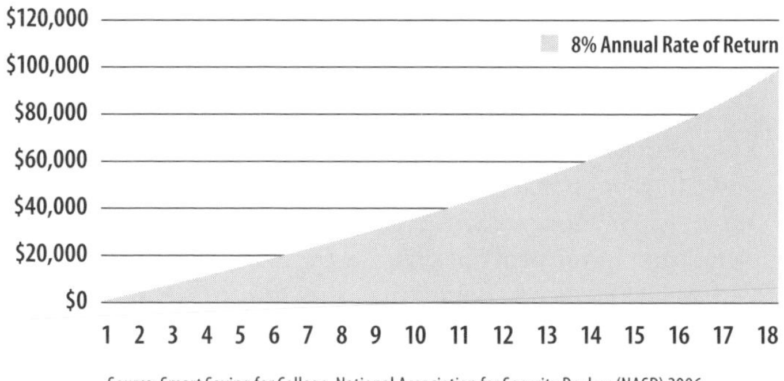

Source: Smart Saving for College, National Association for Security Dealers (NASD) 2006.

Consider Section 529 Plans For College Savings

IRS Section 529 plans are the most preferred form of tax-advantaged savings for college. The Pension Reform Act of 2006 makes withdrawals from 529 plans permanently tax-free when used by the beneficiary for qualified educational expenses (including tuition, fees, room and board). Prior to the Pension Reform Act of 2006, the tax-free withdrawal status granted to 529 plans was scheduled to expire in 2010, giving some hesitation to invest in 529 plans beyond 2010 due to tax treatment uncertainties. *Now that this issue has been resolved, 529 plans are the best option for college savings for most families.*

There are two types of 529 plans. The first involves prepaid tuition options. These plans allow you to lock in the cost of college tuition at your state's public universities at a rate determined in today's dollars. You can either finance the entire tuition purchase in one lump sum or through installment payments. Check with your state's 529 prepaid college tuition program to determine the options available for purchase. These programs generally require either you or the child beneficiary to be a resident of the state where the program is administered. (Note that prepaid college tuition plans are not available in every state.)

The second type of 529 plan (and most widely used 529 plan) is referred to as a *college savings plan*. This type of 529 plan allows direct investment in a variety of mutual funds administered by a host of mutual fund companies. A good place to find the 529 plan options offered by your state and to view 529 plans sponsored by other states can be located at saving for college.com (www.savingforcollege.com). This site provides a wealth of information regarding state-sponsored 529 plans and includes links to each state's 529 plan administrators.

Check with your state's 529 college savings plan to find out if your state offers income tax incentives to enroll in your state's 529 sponsored program. Unlike prepaid tuition programs sponsored by some states, you do not need to enroll in your state's sponsored college savings plan. That's why it's important to look at college savings programs sponsored by other states. You might find a college savings plan sponsored by another state that offers the investment options that best fit your college savings plan goals. Distributions from each state-sponsored plan can be transferred to any public or private university of your choice. Contribution limits (minimums and maximums) are set by each plan. Since this is a defined contribution type plan, the biggest risk is that funds accumulated in the account will not be sufficient to pay for all qualified educational expenses. That's why it's important to establish a systematic savings program and to choose mutual funds (stock and bond funds or target funds) that deliver a respectable annualized return.

When choosing a 529 college savings plan, be sure to read the fund's prospectus to find out the fees and investment objectives of the fund. If choosing a 529 option on your own, be sure to choose an option that is *no-load and charges annual fees of less than 1% of asset value.* If working with a financial advisor, a mutual fund load might make sense based on the advice you've received from your advisor and the performance of the fund you've selected. There are no income restrictions for single and married taxpayers to make annual contributions to 529 plans.

Other Tax-Advantaged College Plans & U.S. Savings Bonds

- **Coverdell Education Savings Accounts**—this type of plan created in 1997 was formerly known as an Education IRA. These plans also enjoy the same tax-deferred advantages as 529 plans. However, annual contribution maximums are lower and cannot exceed $2,000 per beneficiary per year. A big advantage of Coverdell Accounts is that money invested in these plans can be used for Kindergarten through 12th grade expenses, giving them additional flexibility versus 529 college savings plans. However, this flexibility is scheduled to expire in 2010, unless extended by Congress. In addition, there are income limitations for single and married taxpayers. Single taxpayers are not allowed to make contributions to the account if modified adjusted gross income exceeds $110,000. Married taxpayers' modified adjusted gross income cannot exceed $220,000. Based on Coverdell's lower contribution limits and income restrictions, most people will find a 529 plan to be a better option for higher education saving.

- **Custodial Accounts**—these are Uniform Gift to Minors Act (UGMA) accounts or Uniform Transfer to Minors Act (UTMA) accounts. These accounts allow the first $750 in annual earnings to be tax-free. For children under the age of 14, the next $750 is taxed at the child's tax rate. Any annual earnings above $1,500 are taxed at the custodian's (who is usually the parent) tax rate. Once the child reaches age 14, the first $750 in annual earnings remains tax-free and all earnings above $750 are taxed at the child's tax rate.

  One big disadvantage of custodial accounts is control of ownership. Once the account is established, any money accumulated in the account legally belongs to the beneficiary. Once the child reaches the age of majority from 18 to 25 years of age (defined by each state), he or she takes control of the account and can use the money for any purpose. This makes this type of account generally a weaker choice than a 529 or Coverdell option, because these plans allow for custodial control of assets after the plans are established. Custodial account beneficiaries cannot be changed once elected. With both 529 and Coverdell plans, beneficiaries can be changed at the discretion of the custodian.

- **Series EE and I Savings Bonds**—interest from these bonds is tax-free for state and local income taxes and can also avoid federal income taxation when used for qualified higher education expenses. Modified adjusted gross income cannot exceed certain limits for interest to avoid federal taxation (see IRS Publication 970 for additional details). Some organizations offer payroll deduction for purchase of these types of savings bonds. For some people, this may represent a convenient way to accumulate college funds over time. However, since you will need significantly more growth in your investments than savings bonds produce, make sure to limit your overall investment in savings bonds to less than 25% of the projected amount needed for college expenses.

Applying For Financial Aid

Apply early for financial aid. Start by completing the Free Application for Federal Student Aid (FAFSA) in January of the school year applying for aid. For example, for the 2009-2010 school year, which begins in August or September 2009, apply in January 2009 for the best opportunity to get financial aid. You can fill out an application online at www.fafsa.ed.gov. You can also receive the FAFSA form by calling FAFSA's toll free number, 1-800-433-3243. It's essential to complete the FAFSA report timely, because both public and private colleges rely on the results of this report to calculate student financial aid awards. Here are some of the key items that will be produced from your FAFSA report:

- **The Student Aid Report**—this report summarizes the information provided in the FAFSA and lists your Expected Family Contribution (EFC). The EFC is the amount your family is expected to contribute during the school year for college costs. This report will also let you know if you qualify for a federal Pell Grant. Pell grant awards do not need to be repaid when used for college expenses.
- **Eligibility for other types of aid programs**—these include Perkins Loans, Stafford Loans and college work-study programs. Choose federal government-sponsored Perkins and Stafford loans over privately-sponsored college loans due to their fixed interest rates and lower interest charges over the life of the loan.

Some private schools may require the completion of additional supplemental forms to make a financial aid determination. They may require the completion of the College Board's College Scholarship Service (CSS) profile, formerly known as the FAF. There is a fee for each school selected to receive the CSS report. Check with the financial aid office to determine the forms needed and the deadline for receipt of aid forms. Each college will likely have slightly different deadlines so make sure you know the appropriate deadlines to ensure the best opportunity to secure limited scholarship and aid funds.

A great source to help you navigate through the complexity of college aid filing can be found at the National Association of Student Financial Aid Administrators' website: www.finaid.org. This site is loaded with great ideas for securing college funding. There are a number of excellent financial calculators on this site that will help you to get an idea of college costs. One of the calculators will also give you an estimate of your Expected Family Contribution for college expenses. By using this calculator, you'll get an idea of how much financial aid departments will expect your family to contribute to the overall cost of a year of college.

Carefully Evaluate Financial Aid Packages

Evaluate the financial aid "package" offered by each college. Balance the overall financial package with the attributes of the schools being considered. The best financial aid packages have grants and scholarships. These generally don't need to be repaid. Loans will need to be repaid upon graduation. *Make sure that the loan amounts don't saddle you, your child or dependent with too much debt upon graduation.* This is where trade-offs will need to be made based on each college's curriculum and overall cost projections. That's why it makes sense during the application process to choose a variety of public and private colleges for consideration. Just because a private college will cost more than a public college, scholarship awards and other grants may make the private school less costly than a public institution. It's best to "cast a wide net" when evaluating colleges to find the best educational value. Like any other long-term purchase, the lowest cost is seldom the best value when it comes to education.

College costs represent a significant investment in the growth and development of yourself or a dependent. *Make sure you take the time to find a college that meets your (and your dependent's) goals, educational objectives and your budget.*

Charitable Giving

Overall financial wellness is enhanced when we carefully give our time, talents and a portion of our finances to worthy organizations or causes. For those who belong to a church, synagogue, mosque, or other religious organization, there are generally established guidelines for financial giving and there are ample opportunities to share with others any special talents you may have. For others who do not participate in organized religion (and for those who do), the number of worthy causes is almost overwhelming. The easiest way to give to many needy organizations in your local community is through gifts to your local United Way agency. Also consider direct contributions to organizations that you find worthwhile. If finances are tight, consider gifts of time. Most benevolent organizations are in dire need of committed volunteers, and volunteering also helps you to plug in socially with like-minded people.

Take the time to list organizations that are important to you. *A good rule of thumb is to set aside anywhere from 5% to 15% of your income to give to a variety of charitable or benevolent causes.* If you find that you have too much consumer debt, lighten up on your financial contributions, but try to give more of your time and talents to causes that you deem worthy. As your finances improve throughout life, you should direct a portion of your income to fund the causes that are important to you. Life is all about proper balance and charitable giving should truly become a long-term strategy in your pursuit of overall lifelong financial wellness.

Take the time to review and complete the *Action Step Checklist* on the following page. Also refer to **Appendices 8-1** through **8-4** and take the time to list your important goals. This exercise will help you to identify the goals that have the most importance to you during your journey toward long-term financial wellness.

Let's now move to **Step #9** in our journey toward financial wellness. In this chapter we will review why it is important to seek wise counsel on matters related to legal, financial and insurance needs. Having the services of trusted, competent counsel is an essential ingredient in obtaining lifelong financial wellness...

8
ACTION STEP CHECKLIST

Step #8 Action Step Checklist

Congratulations on completing Step #8. Listed are some key Action Steps to consider from this chapter. When you've finished the Action Step, place a ✓ next to the Step to document your progress.

Here is your Action Step Checklist from Step #8:

- ______Take the time to list your important personal development, career, financial and spiritual or higher purpose goals listed in Appendices 8-1 through 8-4 in the Appendix Section in the back of the book. Make sure your goals are specific and measurable.

- ______The true magic of long-term investing is the power of compound interest. Review Exhibit 8-1. This illustrates how compound interest grows invested amounts over time. When you commit to long-term investing, you get the advantage of compound interest to make your investments grow over a period of years.

- ______Take advantage of IRA options to build tax-deferred or tax-free investment growth for retirement. The two primary IRA options are the Traditional IRA and the Roth IRA.

- ______Higher education (either college or vocational) is a critical component in building long-term financial wellness. With college and vocational education costs rising at a much faster pace than overall inflation, take the time to explore long-term saving and investing options, including 529 prepaid tuition or college savings plans.

- ______Apply early for financial aid for college and vocational training. Aid programs vary considerably from institution to institution. Take the time to carefully evaluate all financial aid packages. Financial aid packages often contain a mix of scholarships, grants, loans and work study options.

- ______Charitable contributions should be carefully considered to ensure that your hard-earned dollars are supporting organizations that are important to you. Make a list of organizations that are important for consideration of a contribution. Rank the importance of organizations to you and give according to your ranking and budget. Also consider gifts of your time and talents to worthwhile charitable organizations.

9

STEP 9
Seek Wise Counsel

"One hour spent with a wise individual can be priceless."

Rely On Wise Counsel

Think of good independent advisors as the "glue" that holds your financial plans and goals together. In this chapter, we'll examine some of the areas where you should seek solid legal, financial and insurance advice. To attain financial wellness, you'll need to work with competent professionals who have specialized knowledge, experience and talents to help you reach your financial goals.
With the explosion of financial services over the past decade, there is plenty of competition for your hard-earned dollars. Avoid the get rich schemes that appear in your mailbox, in your e-mail, on television, (especially those real estate and stock trading infomercials!), on the Internet and over the phone.

The road to financial wellness takes years to navigate and there will be bumps scattered throughout the journey you'll take. Trusted advisors will help you to stay the course or change direction as your financial situation evolves. It's simply too difficult to attain financial wellness completely on your own.

Find A Good Lawyer

A good lawyer can be worth his or her weight in gold when needed. For most of us, we should seek the services of a lawyer who possesses expertise in estate planning and contract law. Proper estate planning is a critical component for long-term financial wellness, yet 58 percent of adults lack a basic will. Equally alarming, 68 percent lack a living will or medical directive that explains an individual's wishes for life support in the event of permanent unconsciousness or a lingering terminal illness.

Even if you are single or just starting your career, take the time to get a basic will that specifies your wishes for distribution of your property at death. Also, make sure that you have a medical directive created for healthcare decisions should you become incapacitated. Store these documents with your attorney, trusted friends or family members or in a safe deposit box for access when needed. Without a will or a medical directive, you are leaving the disposition of your assets and perhaps your medical care decisions (should you become incapacitated) to the state or to family members.

Individuals who die without a will can create havoc with potential heirs to the estate's assets. Each of us probably knows all too well what can happen when family members and the state are left to decide equitable distribution of property. In short, it tends to get very messy for all parties involved. A will and a medical directive solve many of these potential problems.

Remember to keep your will and your medical directive updated. A good time to review these documents is whenever there is a major change in your life such as a marriage, divorce, birth of children, significant accumulation of assets, or major purchase of life insurance. Major life changes often not only necessitate an updating of existing documents but the creation of new estate planning documents such as living trusts. A good attorney will work with you to ensure that your necessary estate documents are sufficient to handle the disposition of your assets and to specify the management of your assets should you become temporarily or permanently incapacitated.

One of the best ways to find the right attorney for your estate planning needs is to consult with friends and associates you trust who have had experience working with attorneys. Good professional sources for attorneys can come from your accountant or from bank trust department officers who specialize in estate planning. Most attorneys will grant at least a telephone consultation at no charge to discuss the scope of your estate planning or legal needs. For basic wills and medical directives, you might be surprised how reasonable these services are, especially when your estate needs are straightforward.

We live in a litigious society. Having a relationship with a competent attorney can help you avoid lawsuits or keep you from entering business or personal financial transactions that you may regret. If you are thinking of ever launching a business (or writing a book!), make sure you consult an attorney to discuss the legal risks you might encounter and to focus on whether the business should be set up as a sole proprietorship, partnership, or some form of incorporation.

Find A Trusted Financial Advisor

Beware of the title *"Financial Planner."* This title is used loosely in the financial services industry. In some cases, a financial planner has just the minimum licensing to sell securities to you, often at very high fees. The Financial Planners Standards Council has developed 10 insightful questions you should ask any financial planner before agreeing to engage in financial planning services. These questions are excellent and the answers to them should give you a level of comfort with the financial planner.

Here are 10 questions to ask when interviewing a financial planner:

1. **What are your qualifications?**
2. **What experience do you have?**
3. **What services do you offer?**
4. **What is your approach to financial planning?**
5. **Will you be the only person working with me?**
6. **How will I pay for your services?**
7. **How much do you typically charge?**
8. **Could anyone besides me benefit from your recommendations?**
9. **Are you regulated by any organization?**
10. **Can I have it in writing?**

Appendix 9-1 (located in the Appendix Section in the back of this book) is a checklist that you can use for interviewing a financial planner. By using this checklist, you'll be in a position to assess the scope of services offered by the financial planner, the planner's experience, educational background, and industry-specific licenses. A good financial planner will keep you on track to reach your financial goals. Your planner should provide objective analysis of your overall financial situation. Once your financial plan has been established, you and your financial planner should determine how often meetings should take place to evaluate your progress.

How Financial Planners Get Paid

Most financial planners will choose one of three methods for payment. The first is fee-based only. At first glance it would appear that fee-only would involve a simple fee for service relationship. But that's not always the case. In fact the CFP Board of Professional Review has laid out specific guidelines for what constitutes a "fee-only" client relationship for those who have the CFP® credential. The acceptable fee-only compensation arrangements include:

- Hourly, fixed or flat fees;
- Percentage fees, which are based on some aspect of the client's financial profile, such as assets under management or earned income; and
- Performance-based fees, which are tied to the profitability of the client's invested assets.

When choosing a fee-only planner, make sure you know how the planner will be compensated and to avoid misunderstanding, ask the planner to commit the fee structure in writing.

The second common method for financial planner compensation is through the sale of financial products to you. *There is nothing wrong with this method of compensation, if the financial planner is providing you with solid financial products that fit your unique financial needs.* One advantage of this type of compensation is you don't pay for the planner's time on a direct basis. The planner only gets compensated based on the financial products you purchase. There are excellent financial products that pay financial planners a commission for placing business. Just make sure that your financial planner discloses how he or she is compensated for the products proposed and also look into any up front fees, sometimes called "loads" and ongoing fees for the proposed product. Make sure the planner thoroughly understands your needs before recommending a financial product to fit your unique financial situation. Beware of planners that promote the virtues of variable annuities without assessing how you are currently funding your retirement accounts. Unless you are "maxing out" the available contributions you can make to both your company's retirement plan and an IRA, you probably should not consider a variable annuity.

The third method of compensation is a combination of fee-based and commission-based compensation. Again there is nothing unethical about this type of compensation if it is properly disclosed to you. My parting comment on this form of compensation is that the financial planner better be really good to charge both fixed-fees and to receive commissions from the sale of products! With this type of fee arrangement, you could end up paying a bundle for the services and the financial products your financial planner provides.

Personally, I believe most people are best served when they work with a "fee-based" financial planner who charges either by the hour, project or on the value of the financial assets under management.

Find A Good Insurance Agent

You will need a variety of insurance policies to protect your income and your assets. A top-notch insurance agent is absolutely invaluable. A good agent will guide you in the selection of appropriate insurance coverage levels and will be your point person in the resolution of claims you file for covered events.

Like all professionals, insurance agents vary in their degree of knowledge and commitment to service. If you're in the market for an insurance agent, take the time to meet with at least 3 agents before deciding on an agent for your policies. The best insurance agents will survey your needs, often through a formal questionnaire process to ensure that you have appropriate coverage for a variety of risks, including property and casualty, life, disability, health and long-term care. Beware of agents that want to either take "orders" or have the "one-size fits all" solution to your insurance needs. Some people will find that they are best served in working with more than one insurance agent due to the complex nature of insurance policies. Even the most well-rounded insurance agents will have a difficult time being proficient in all lines of insurance coverage.

To help you find an agent that is best for you, consider the following:

1. **Ask the agent for his/her insurance credentials.** The insurance business provides considerable opportunities for agents to earn industry-specific credentials. Find out if the agent has taken the time to earn insurance designations and find out what the designation covers. There is a literal "alphabet soup" of designations in the insurance industry.

2. **Find out how long the agent has been in the insurance business.** Tenure in the insurance business doesn't always equate to being a good agent, but experience in the business is often a requisite for a good agent.

3. **Ask for references.** This is an important step. Find out from references if they've ever filed a claims and how the agent has been in his or her follow up with claims issues or with questions regarding coverage. Also find out how the agent's professional staff performs. A good professional staff is also critical for good servicing.

4. **Find out if the agent is captive or independent.** A captive agent represents one company, like State Farm, Allstate, etc. Captive agents can only represent the policies that their company offers. Conversely, an independent agent will usually represent a number of insurance carriers. Which one is best? It depends. There are some unique advantages and disadvantages associated with captive or independent insurance agents. A captive agent should provide a much higher level of policy coordination since multiple policies are handled through the same carrier. Conversely, an independent agent may be able to secure better pricing and servicing through the placement of insurance business through more than one insurance carrier.

5. **Select an agent you trust.** Trust is something that is earned. Look for an agent who listens to your needs and puts your unique needs first and foremost when selecting insurance coverage. Trust your "gut" instincts and perform due diligence when choosing an agent. A good agent should be a long-term partner in your quest for financial wellness.

Finding Insurance Without an Agent

For most people, choosing insurance without the services of a trusted advisor is a mistake. It's not prudent for most people to go direct to an insurer for coverage because knowing how much insurance to purchase can be tricky, especially for those who do not have exposure to the insurance industry. However, if you decide to go direct to the insurance carrier for any type of insurance, make sure you know what you are buying and understand how much coverage you need. By going alone, you can save money, but you can also buy too little or too much coverage. If you decide to purchase insurance through direct methods, only purchase insurance coverage for insurance lines that you understand. *If you are at all confused about the coverage you are considering, seek professional insurance agent guidance.*

There are some excellent insurance resources available for the insurance informed, "do-it-yourselfer." For term life insurance, there are a number of insurance companies competing to offer great coverage at a low price. (Be sure to complete **Appendix 7-1** to determine how much life insurance you'll need.) You can find a host of self-service Internet life insurance brokers like SelectQuote (selectquote.com) or for automobile and property and casualty insurance there are direct insurers like Geico (geico.com) or Progressive (progressive.com) for consideration. If you've decided to purchase insurance on your own, take the time to get several quotes from reputable insurance carriers and take the time to know the details of your purchased coverage.

Print out everything related to the policies being considered so that you know the specific policy coverage, policy limitations and specific exclusions. A key to long-term financial wellness is having the right amount of insurance to cover the financial risks that can occur during your lifetime. *Being underinsured in such areas as life, disability, health, home and auto coverage can expose you to undue financial risk.* Remember that insurance is designed to protect the assets you have from unforeseen financial risks. Having the proper level of insurance is something you'll need to monitor throughout your life.

Find A Good Realtor®

Your home may be your single largest investment. In real estate the worn cliché of the importance of location, location, location is so true. A good Realtor can help you find not only the best location for your budget, but can also help you avoid buying pitfalls when purchasing property. A key element to finding a good Realtor is through personal references and through an interview. I'm amazed at how little time some people take when choosing a Realtor. Once you start working with a Realtor, especially if you list the house with a Realtor, you are "locked in" for a period of time (usually 3 to 6 months) before you can make a switch to a new agent.

Whenever you are seeking to buy or sell a property, know who the Realtor represents. There are buyers' agents and sellers' agents. When looking for a home, make sure you sign an agreement with a Realtor to serve as your agent, making the agent a "buyers' agent." This is critical, because absent an agreement with a Realtor to represent you as a buyers' agent, you could find that the Realtor may need to represent the interests of the seller of the property first and foremost, resulting in a potential compromise of your negotiating power when entering into a real estate transaction. When selling a property, the agent you list with is by definition a sellers' agent. As a result, the sellers' agent is obligated to represent your best interest as the seller of the property.

Like all professionals, some Realtors are much better suited to serve your unique purchase and sale needs than others. Certainly personal references are a good place to start in finding a good Realtor to represent your purchase or sale needs. In addition, you should always take the time to interview at least 3 Realtors before listing your home or before entering into an agreement to have the Realtor serve as your buyers' agent. Here are some questions to ask a prospective Realtor during the interview process:

- **How long has the agent been in real estate sales and how many homes has the agent sold in the last year?** You want to make sure you are working with a full-time agent who has had a level of success in your market.

- **How will the agent market your home or find a home for you?** You can find out a lot about the relative quality and marketing savvy of the agent by finding out how he or she will actively advertise and promote your home, if selling. If you are looking for a home with a buyers' agent, you'll find out the specific steps the Realtor will take to find a home that meets your financial and location criteria. Be sure to hold your Realtor to implementation of the promised promotional program for your home after you've agreed to list your home. This is one way to ensure that you get the most from the Realtor you've selected to list your home.

- **Has the agent sold or found homes similar to the one you are seeking?** Assuming the answer is yes, get the names of the agent's clients and make sure you contact them to find out how satisfied they are with the job the agent did for them.

- **Is the Realtor part of a solid agency with a good reputation?** Find out about the agency the Realtor represents. Find out how many homes the entire agency has listed and sold over the past year and how this compares to the number of listings and sales in the area you are considering. You want to choose a Realtor and an agency that is experienced buying or selling homes in an area you are considering.

Selling A Property By Owner

Selling property can be complex, especially if you've not had previous experience in a real estate transaction. Ask anyone who has sold a property on his or her own and they'll tell you that there is a lot more to it than just putting a For Sale sign in the front lawn. You'll need to first know how much your property is worth. *I'd recommend an independent appraisal of your property's value by a licensed independent property appraiser.* You'll spend a few hundred dollars for this service, but it will minimize a key risk you have when listing your home on your own and it's listing your home above or below its market value.

I've generally found that an independent appraisal provides most homeowners with a needed dose of reality with regard to how much their home is worth. By evaluating your home and the prices that comparable homes have sold for in your neighborhood, a good appraiser will give you a good assessment on the price range to consider for listing your home.

Consider setting a deadline for the sale of your home before listing with a Realtor. A good rule to consider (assuming you are not in too much of a rush to sell) is to find out the average amount of time it takes to sell a home in your market. If you've not sold your home within the average selling timeframe, it might make sense to consider listing your home with a Realtor or adjusting your price or rethinking your home marketing strategy.

Unless you are in a red-hot real estate market, you'll need to market your home to introduce it to potential buyers. You'll have to spend money to do this. Consider placing a photo of your home in the local newspaper, along with the unique features of your home and indicate that your home can be viewed by appointment. Also consider making either a flat dollar amount or a percentage of the sale available to any Realtors who bring you a qualified buyer. Be sure to negotiate the dollar amount that you will pay to a Realtor for bringing you a buyer. This can make good sense, because the amount you'll pay a Realtor for bringing you a qualified buyer should be half or less what you'd pay to formally list your property with a real estate agency, where commissions can range from 5 to 7 percent of the sale price.

Good Advisors Are Worth Their Fees

We all have unique talents and experiences that help us in life. Some people will find that they are adept in buying insurance, real estate and other complex business transactions with little or no guidance. For those with the unique skills to do this, savings are often realized. *However, the majority of people are much better served by taking the time to hire an objective expert in selecting insurance coverage and purchasing or selling real estate.* Sure, it may appear that the costs are too high, especially when selling real estate. But recognize that good professional advisors should be able to add value in a number of ways by getting you a higher price from the sale of your real estate than you could possibly negotiate on your own or by getting you the best insurance coverage for the premium paid.

Having a trusted circle of competent legal, financial and insurance advisors is a necessary step for most people to take when pursuing lifelong financial wellness. Take the time to make sure that you have the best team of professionals assembled to help you with your legal, insurance and financial matters. By having the right team serving you, giving you the latest and best information for your legal, financial and insurance needs, you'll more than likely come out ahead of those who try to do most of this critical work on their own.

Take the time to review and complete the *Action Step Checklist* on the following page.

In the next and final Step on our journey toward lifelong financial wellness, we'll tie together the concepts that we've covered in this and in previous chapters to ensure that you are on solid ground to achieving long-term financial wellness in your life…

9
ACTION STEP CHECKLIST

Step #9 Action Step Checklist

Congratulations on completing Step #9. Listed are some key Action Steps to consider from this chapter. When you've finished the Action Step, place a ✓ next to the Step to document your progress.

Here is your Action Step Checklist from Step #9:

- ______Rely on wise counsel to help you navigate your journey toward financial wellness. Take the time to find an attorney to handle your necessary legal document preparation (wills, durable power of attorney for healthcare, etc.). An independent financial advisor can help you maintain the discipline to reach your financial goals. Consider using Appendix 9-1 as a checklist for interviewing a financial planner. Other trusted professionals that can provide invaluable advice include insurance agents and Realtors.

- ______Before moving forward with the services of a financial advisor, make sure you know how your advisor is compensated for his/her services. You will generally get the most objective advice from a financial advisor who charges fees based on an hourly or fixed-fee basis.

- ______When selecting any professional for advice, take the time to research qualifications, including education, experience and credentials (such as CFP, CLU, CPA, etc.). A good source for finding competent advisors is to ask people you know and respect who they'd recommend for the task at hand. Always ask for and check references to make sure that the professional is serving his/her clients appropriately.

- ______If you wish to purchase insurance on a direct basis, make sure you know what you are buying to avoid being under or over-insured.

- ______A good Realtor can be an invaluable partner in selling your home at the right price, including the myriad details associated with selling your home. If you work with a Realtor, make sure that he/she presents and implements a solid marketing plan for your property. If you decide to sell your home on your own, get an independent property appraisal and establish a timeframe for sale. If this timeframe passes, be sure to consider securing the services of a Realtor to assist in the sale of your home.

10

STEP 10
Tying It All Together

"Do it now."

THIS WILL BE THE SHORTEST CHAPTER IN THE BOOK. It's the shortest chapter for a reason. My 10th and final step can be summed up in three words: ***Do It Now!*** *No matter your age or your income, you now can unlock the awesome power of financial wellness in your life!* Repeat: ***Do It Now!*** By implementing the specific Steps outlined in this book, you'll give yourself the best shot at attaining the 10th and final step in your journey: *Financial Wellness.* But you must implement the key Steps outlined in this book for the 10th and final Step to become a reality in your life. Every Step that I've listed in this book will help you to build a solid financial foundation. I've followed each Step in my life and the result has had a profound impact on my overall wellness. It has allowed me to make career and personal decisions that have improved my overall well-being and have improved the lives of those who depend on me. I'm convinced that you can experience the awesome gift that financial wellness will bring in your life by following the Steps in this book.

I'd like to offer a special "congratulations" to you for completing the previous nine chapter Steps in this book. Getting through any book, especially with our time-starved schedules, takes an investment in precious time and effort. Your efforts will be rewarded when you follow the principles outlined in each chapter Step. To maximize the impact of this book, be sure to keep it handy as a reference guide throughout your journey toward financial wellness. There will be Steps that you'll need to revisit from time to time depending on your personal circumstances.

Following Each Step Will Enhance Your Life

Each chapter is designed to give you specific Steps that you can take to achieve financial wellness in your life. Some of these Steps may have been new territory for you to explore and other chapter Steps may have reinforced what you already know and are practicing in your life. There may be other principles outlined in the book that make you seek more information before making an important financial decision. When you gather more information about matters related to your finances, it will often serve you well. Just be sure to get advice from solid, objective sources and never rush into commitments involving your finances.

I hope this book has reinforced the fact that financial wellness is ultimately your responsibility and it will not be provided exclusively by your employer or the government. When you actively apply the principles outlined in this book, you'll put into motion a proactive set of forces that will lead you on a systematic path in the direction of long-term financial wellness.

Financial Wellness Will Change Your Life

So how do you know when you've attained financial wellness? Chances are you'll realize slowly, over time, that you are gaining control over areas involving your finances that once seemed daunting in your life. You'll discover the peace of mind that comes from gaining control over your finances. You'll start to eliminate debt, focus your spending priorities and you'll establish a solid foundation for your long-term investments. This will prove to be empowering and your accomplishments will lead to other successes in your journey to build long-term financial wellness. *Success breeds success.*

You'll begin to develop a "mindset" that will lead you to triumph in other areas of your financial life. You'll find that financial wellness will have a positive impact on your career and your personal relationships. When you are in control of your finances instead of your finances being in control of you, you'll make career decisions that complement your financial wellness objectives. You'll also have more precious time to devote to others. I believe that we are truly "financially well" when we can have a positive impact on people and organizations that really matter to us. By attaining financial wellness, the giving back that you'll probably do with your time and resources to others will result in a tremendous payoff in personal satisfaction.

Financial wellness will allow you to live each season of life knowing that you can weather most of the inevitable changes that will confront you. You'll look at your career differently. You'll realize that your career no longer defines who you are or what you can or can't do. It's a great mindset to possess and it will open your eyes to the opportunities and possibilities that exist in our world of fast-paced changes and unlimited opportunities. Financial wellness will improve your life and the lives of those you have the pleasure to serve.

Knowledge Is Power

I wrote this book to show you that financial wellness can be achieved by most people with the right knowledge, effort and the discipline to follow the Steps outlined in this book. *You can do this.* It doesn't take an advanced degree in financial management or a high income to build a rock-solid financial foundation to achieve long-term financial wellness. It takes discipline and the desire to control your finances with careful planning and the use of time to achieve your goals.

We now live in a global economy where you must take action to secure your financial future. One of the best ways to do this is to take full advantage of company-sponsored benefit plans, especially saving plans like 401(k), 403(b) or 457 plans. Take the time to know what your employer offers as part of its benefits package. *Make employer-sponsored savings plans a key component to your long-term savings and investment strategy.* The tax benefits of this strategy, the ease of systematic saving through payroll deduction and the fact that Social Security and Medicare benefits will likely shrink in the future make it even more important than ever to save and invest in plans offered through your employer. Saving and investing through employer-sponsored retirement accounts and through IRAs will allow you to harness the awesome accumulating power of compound interest.

Take the time to review and complete the final *Action Step Checklist* on the following page. Make it a point to periodically refer to each chapter Step's *Action Step Checklist* so that you stay on track in your journey toward long-term financial wellness.

I hope this book will change not only your life but the lives of those who depend on you. Taking the Steps to attain financial wellness will truly add a special dimension to your life. Any worthwhile journey starts with a series of disciplined Steps. Through *The 10 Steps To Financial Wellness* you now have the roadmap to experience the joy financial wellness can bring to your life. *Enjoy the journey!*

ACTION STEP CHECKLIST

Step #10 Action Step Checklist

Congratulations on completing Step #10—the final Step in this book! Listed are some key Action Steps to consider from this chapter and book. When you've finished the Action Step, place a ✓ next to the Step to document your progress.

Here is your Final Action Step Checklist:

- ______Now that you've taken the time to go through all 10 Steps in this book, make a commitment to get started in building financial wellness in your life. Remember that procrastination is your biggest enemy in this process. That's why it's important to start this process **NOW**.

- ______Follow the Chapter Steps and you'll give yourself the best opportunity to attain financial wellness. The principles outlined in each Step are time-tested and should guide you in your journey.

- ______Complete the Action Step Checklist that appears at the end of each chapter Step. This will help you to systematically implement key principles outlined in the chapter.

- ______Be sure to refer often to the Appendix Section in the back of the book. In this section you'll find invaluable budgeting, cash flow and checklist information that will enhance your financial wellness. Take the time to complete your Personal Net Worth Statement and Your Monthly Cash Flow Statement (found in **Appendices 1-1** and **1-2**). These will serve as the first major benchmarks in the overall measurement of your financial wellness.

- ______Keep this book handy in an easy-to-reference area. You'll likely find that it will prove helpful when you need information on an issue that this book covers.

- ______Understand that financial wellness can be attained through careful planning and through making good financial and personal choices. **Remember: Do It Now!**

Appendix

Appendix 1-1—Personal Financial Net Worth Statement

Assets

Taxable Investments	**Current Value**
1. Cash—include checking, savings accounts, CDs, money market accounts	$__________
2. Stocks, bonds and mutual funds	$__________
3. Investments in real estate (do not include your home)	$__________
4. Value in businesses privately held	$__________
5. Value of other taxable investments	$__________
Tax-Advantaged Investments	
6. Value of 401(k), 403(b) or 457 accounts	$__________
7. Value of defined benefit pension plan (if applicable)	$__________
8. Value of IRAs and self employment plans (SEPs & Keoghs)	$__________
9. Value of education savings accounts (529 plans, UGMA)	$__________
10. Variable annuity plans	$__________
11. Other tax-advantaged investments	$__________
Personal Property	
12. Approximate market value of primary residence	$__________
13. Other properties including second homes	$__________
14. Value of home furnishings	$__________
15. Value of automobiles, if owned	$__________
16. Other	$__________
17. Total Assets (add lines 1-16)	$__________

Debts

18. Mortgage balance $__________
19. Home equity loans $__________
20. Credit card balances $__________
21. Student loans $__________
22. Automobile loans or lease payments $__________
23. Other debt $__________
24. Total Debt (add lines 18-23) $__________

Financial Net Worth: Line 17 minus line 24. **$__________**

Appendix 1-2—Monthly Cash Flow Budget/Worksheet

Adopted From Financial Planning at About.com

CATEGORY	Budget Amount	Actual Amount	Difference
INCOME			
Take home pay			
Interest Income			
Investment Income			
Miscellaneous Income			
***TOTAL INCOME:			
EXPENSES	**Budget Amount**	**Actual Amount**	**Difference**
HOME			
Mortgage or Rent			
Homeowners/Renters Insurance			
Property Taxes			
Home Repairs/Maintenance/HOA Dues			
Home Improvements			
UTILITIES			
Electricity			
Water and Sewer			
Natural Gas or Oil			
Telephone (Land Line, Cell)			
FOOD			
Groceries			
Eating Out, Lunches, Snacks			
FAMILY OBLIGATIONS			
Child Support/Alimony			
Day Care, Baby-sitting			
HEALTH AND MEDICAL			
Insurance (medical, dental, vision)			
Out-of-Pocket Medical Expenses			
Fitness (Yoga, Massage, Gym)			

EXPENSES	Budget Amount	Actual Amount	Difference
TRANSPORTATION			
Car Payments			
Gasoline/Oil			
Auto Repairs/Maintenance/Fees			
Auto Insurance			
Other (tolls, bus, subway, taxi)			
CLOTHING PURCHASES			
DEBT PAYMENTS			
Credit Cards			
Student Loans			
Other Loans			
ENTERTAINMENT/RECREATION			
Cable TV/Videos/Movies			
Computer Expense			
Hobbies			
Subscriptions and Dues			
Vacations			
PETS			
Food			
Grooming, Boarding, Vet			
MISCELLANEOUS			
Toiletries, Household Products			
Gifts/Donations			
Grooming (Hair, Make-up, Other)			
Miscellaneous Expense			
INVESTMENTS AND SAVINGS			
401(K), 403(B) or IRA			
Stocks/Bonds/Mutual Funds			
College Fund			
Savings			
Emergency Fund			
*****TOTAL EXPENSES, INVESTMENTS AND SAVINGS:**			
CASH FLOW SHORTAGE/SURPLUS (TOTAL INCOME MINUS TOTAL EXPENSES, INVESTMENTS AND SAVINGS)			

Appendix 5-1

IRS Code Section 213(d)(1) defines medical care as amounts paid for the diagnosis, cure, mitigation, treatment, or prevention of disease, or for the purpose of affecting any structure or function of the body. Such expenses must be incurred primarily for the prevention or alleviation of a physical or mental defect or illness.

Acupuncture
Ambulance
Artificial limbs
Artificial teeth
Automobile modifications (hand controls, lifts, etc.)
Birth control pills, devices
Birth prevention surgery
Birthing classes
Braille books & magazines
Breast reconstruction
Care for mental handicap
Chiropractors
Christian Science practitioner
Coinsurance, all family members (the "80/20" cost-sharing of medical bills required by many policies after payment of the deductible)
Contact Lens & Supplies
Contact Lens Protection Plan
Contraception
Copays
Corrective / Support Devices* (special mattress or board)
Cosmetic surgery (only if restorative)*
Costs for physical/mental illness
Crutches
Deductible, all family members
Dental fees (if not cosmetic, e.g. teeth whitening)
Dentures
Diagnostic fees
Drug addiction inpatient treatment
Drug & medical supplies
Eyeglasses, incl exam fee
Fee for practical nurse
Fees of licensed osteopaths
Fertility enhancement
Guide dog
Handicapped persons' schools
Hearing devices & batteries
Home Improvements for approved medical conditions*
Insulin
Laboratory fees
Laser eye surgery
Learning Disability—special school fees
Mentally challenged—special home for
Massage Therapy*
Mileage (transportation costs for medical services)
Obstetrical expenses*
Operations
Orthodontia*
Orthopedic shoes
Over-The-Counter Drugs
Oxygen
Physician fees
Prescribed medicine (includes vitamins and contraceptives)
Prenatal care*
Psychiatrist's care
Psychologist's fees
Routine physicals & other non-diagnostic services
Schools and education, special
Smoking Cessation
Special communications equipment for the deaf
Special education for the blind
Sterilization fees
Surgical fees
Therapeutic care for drug & alcohol addiction
Therapy treatments
Transportation services for medical treatment
Tubal Ligation
Tuition at special school for the handicapped
Vasectomy
Weight Loss* (to treat existing disease)
Wheelchair
Wigs*
X-rays

***Please Note:**
Additional guidance is available for meeting eligibility requirements for reimbursement of this expense. Special rules apply, including a requirement for additional physician-supplied documentation of medical condition!

Internal Revenue Code 213(d)
See IRS Publication 502 *"Medical & Dental Expenses"* for further information. Available on Internet: www.irs.gov/formspubs/index.html

While Publication 502 is a good resource to use, it's important to note that the Code specifically forbids reimbursement of Insurance Premiums and Long-Term Care expenses under a Health FSA.

Appendix 6-1—Bond Mutual Fund Definitions

Bond Funds

Funds with 80% or more of their assets invested in bonds are classified as bond funds. Bond funds are divided into two main groups: taxable bond funds and municipal bond funds. (Note: For all bond funds, maturity figures are used only when duration figures are unavailable.)

Short-Term Government: A fund with at least 90% of its bond portfolio invested in government issues with a duration of greater than or equal to one year and less than 3.5 years, or average effective maturity of greater than or equal to one year and less than four years.

Long-Term Bond: A fund that focuses on corporate and other investment-grade issues with an average duration of more than six years, or an average effective maturity of more than 10 years.

Intermediate-Term Bond: A fund that focuses on corporate, government, foreign or other issues with an average duration of greater than or equal to 3.5 years but less than or equal to six years, or an average effective maturity of more than four years but less than 10 years.

Short-Term Bond: A fund that focuses on corporate and other investment-grade issues with an average duration of more than one year but less than 3.5 years, or an average effective maturity of more than one year but less than four years.

Ultra short Bond: Used for funds with an average duration or an average effective maturity of less than one year. This category includes general- and government-bond funds, and excludes any international, convertible, multisector, and high-yield bond funds.

International Bond: A fund that invests at least 40% of bonds in foreign markets.

Emerging-Markets Bond: at least 65% assets in emerging-markets bonds.

High-Yield Bond: A fund with at least 65% of assets in junk bonds (those rated below BBB.)

Multisector Bond: Used for funds that seek income by diversifying their assets among several fixed-income sectors, usually U.S. government obligations, foreign bonds, and high-yield domestic debt securities.

Municipal National Long-Term: A national fund with an average duration of more than seven years, or average maturity of more than 12 years.

Municipal National Intermediate-Term: A national fund with an average duration of more than 4.5 years but less than seven years, or average maturity of more than five years but less than 12 years.

Municipal New York Long-Term: A fund with at least 80% of assets in New York municipal debt, with average duration of more than seven years, or an average maturity of more than 12 years.

Municipal New York Intermediate-Term: A fund with at least 80% of assets in New York municipal debt, with an average duration of between 4.5 years and seven years.

Municipal Single-State Long-Term: A single-state fund with an average duration of more than seven years, or average maturity of more than 12 years.

Municipal Single-State Intermediate-Term: A single-state fund with an average duration of more than 4.5 years but less than seven years, or average maturity of more than five years but less than 12 years.

Municipal Bond Short-Term (national and single state): A fund that focuses on municipal debt/bonds with an average duration of less than 4.5 years, or an average maturity of less than five years.

Source: Morningstar, Inc. (www.morningstar.com)

Appendix 6-2—Stock Mutual Fund Definitions

Domestic-stock funds

Funds with at least 70% of assets in domestic stocks are categorized based on the style and size of the stocks they typically own. The style and size divisions reflect those used in the Morningstar investment style box: value, blend, or growth style and small, medium, or large median market capitalization.

Based on their investment style over the past three years, domestic-stock funds are placed in one of the nine categories: *large growth, large blend, large value, medium growth, medium blend, medium value, small growth, small blend, small value.*

Domestic-equity funds that specialize in a particular sector of the market are placed in a specialty category: communications, financials, healthcare, natural resources, precious metals, real estate, technology, utilities, convertible bond, and domestic hybrid. (Precious-metals funds are assigned star ratings in the international-stock asset class.)

International-Stock Funds

Stock funds that have invested 40% or more of their equity holdings in foreign stocks (on average over the past three years) are placed in an international-stock category.

Europe: at least 75% of stocks invested in Europe.

Japan: at least 75% of stocks invested in Japan.

Latin America: at least 75% of stocks invested in Latin America.

Diversified Pacific: at least 65% of stocks invested in Pacific countries, with at least an additional 10% of stocks invested in Japan.

Asia/Pacific ex-Japan: at least 75% of stocks invested in Pacific countries, with less than 10% of stocks invested in Japan.

Diversified Emerging Markets: at least 50% of stocks invested in emerging markets.

Foreign: an international fund having no more than 10% of stocks invested in the United States.

World: an international fund having more than 10% of stocks invested in the United States. International Hybrid: used for funds with stock holdings of greater than 20% but less than 70% of the portfolio where 40% of the stocks and bonds are foreign.

Source: Morningstar, Inc. (www.morningstar.com)

Appendix 6-3—Exchange Traded Fund (ETF) Information

The chart below indicates some of the characteristics of ETFs. This "hybrid" type investment has characteristics of individual securities (they're traded on financial market exchanges), but also offer the diversification advantages of mutual funds.

UNIQUE CHARACTERISTICS OF ETFS

ETFs are index funds or trusts that are listed and traded intraday on an exchange. ETFs are constructed like Mutual Funds, but trade like stocks. ETFs allow investors to buy or sell an entire portfolio of stocks as a single security. The benefits of ETFs vs. Mutual Funds are as follows:

Attribute	ETFs	Mutual Funds
Diversification	x	x
Continuous pricing	x	
Can be sold short	x	
Can be bought on margin	x	
Can use stop and limit orders	x	
Lower expense ratios	x	Some
Tax Efficient	x	Some

Appendix 7-1—Life Insurance Needs Estimate

- **Calculate the amount of all personal debt including mortgage debt**—add up the value of everything you owe. Most people want to ensure that they leave "this world" with no debt.

  Total: $ _______________

- **Estimate the cost of raising minor children**—according to *Consumer Reports*, the cost of raising a child from birth to age 18 in 2005 for a family earning $70,200 per year is (I hope you are seated!) $353,000, or about $19,611 per year. This does not include the cost of college! These extra costs are calculated in the next step.

  Total: $ _______________

- **Determine the cost of a four year college**—cost for room, board, tuition and fees is expected to be about $130,000 in the year 2021 to complete a four year college education. Double this amount for private college tuition and fees.[12] The College Board estimated the average cost of public college tuition, room and board expenses for the 2005-2006 school year at $12,127; private college tuition, room and board expenses are estimated at $28,655. Add 8.25 percent annual inflation for college expenses beyond the 2005-2006 school year to determine how much you'll need to save for minor children.

  Total: $ _______________

- **Anticipate the annual income needs of spouse or guardian**—estimate how much income your spouse or guardian will need for living expenses on an annual basis and multiply this result by a factor of 10.

  Total: $ _______________

Add the total from each item above.

Subtotal: $ _______________

Subtract from the above **Subtotal** the value of your assets, **(but exclude the value of your home because your home will not generate income)** personal investments, amounts set aside for children in education accounts, the death benefit of life insurance policies in force and the value of retirement accounts.

Total Assets: $ (_________ **)**
Subtract from Subtotal amount

Insurance Est: $ __________
This is the "approximate" amount of life insurance you need.

The result will give you a rough estimate of how much life insurance you'll need. For people with young families, this can be a sizable amount of life insurance! For families with extensive life insurance needs, **term life insurance** can protect your insurance requirements for a reasonable payment, assuming you don't have any serious health issues.

Appendix 8-1—Personal Development Goals

One of the best ways to attain goals is to take the time to write them and refer to them on a periodic basis. During the review process, some goals may cease to be relevant or perhaps they've been attained. Also, new goals will materialize. It's important to keep your goals **current** and **measurable**. Whenever possible, establish a time deadline for attainment of the listed goal. Open-ended timeframes on goal setting can hinder your progress.

Personal Development Goals (list goals that are important to you and specify a timeframe for completion—1 year, 3 years, 5 years, etc.)

Goal # 1 (list goal)

____

Why is goal important to you?________________________________

Timeframe for completion of goal? ____________________________

Goal # 2 (list goal)

____

Why is goal important to you?________________________________

Timeframe for completion of goal? ____________________________

Goal # 3 (list goal)

____

Why is goal important to you?________________________________

Timeframe for completion of goal? ____________________________

Use This Format to List Additional Goals on a Separate Document if Needed

Appendix 8-2—Career Goals

One of the best ways to attain goals is to take the time to write them and refer to them on a periodic basis. During the review process, some goals may cease to be relevant or perhaps they've been attained. Also, new goals will materialize. It's important to keep your goals **current** and **measurable**. Whenever possible, establish a time deadline for attainment of the listed goal. Open-ended timeframes on goal setting can hinder your progress.

Career Goals (list goals that are important to you and specify a timeframe for completion—1 year, 3 years, 5 years, etc.)

Goal # 1 (list goal)

____

Why is goal important to you? ______________________________

Timeframe for completion of goal? ___________________________

Goal # 2 (list goal)

____

Why is goal important to you? ______________________________

Timeframe for completion of goal? ___________________________

Goal # 3 (list goal)

____

Why is goal important to you? ______________________________

Timeframe for completion of goal? ___________________________

Use This Format to List Additional Goals on a Separate Document if Needed

Appendix 8-3—Financial Goals

One of the best ways to attain goals is to take the time to write them and refer to them on a periodic basis. During the review process, some goals may cease to be relevant or perhaps they've been attained. Also, new goals will materialize. It's important to keep your goals **current** and **measurable**. Whenever possible, establish a time deadline for attainment of the listed goal. Open-ended timeframes on goal setting can hinder your progress.

Financial Goals (list goals that are important to you and specify a timeframe for completion—1 year, 3 years, 5 years, etc.)

Goal # 1 (list goal)

____

Why is goal important to you?_______________________________

Timeframe for completion of goal? ___________________________

Goal # 2 (list goal)

____

Why is goal important to you?_______________________________

Timeframe for completion of goal? ___________________________

Goal # 3 (list goal)

____

Why is goal important to you?_______________________________

Timeframe for completion of goal? ___________________________

Use This Format to List Additional Goals on a Separate Document if Needed

Appendix 8-4—Spiritual or Higher Purpose Goals

One of the best ways to attain goals is to take the time to write them and refer to them on a periodic basis. During the review process, some goals may cease to be relevant or perhaps they've been attained. Also, new goals will materialize. It's important to keep your goals **current** and **measurable**. Whenever possible, establish a time deadline for attainment of the listed goal. Open-ended timeframes on goal setting can hinder your progress.

Spiritual or Higher Purpose Goals (list goals that are important to you and specify a timeframe for completion—1 year, 3 years, 5 years, etc.)

Goal # 1 (list goal)

____

Why is goal important to you? ______________________

Timeframe for completion of goal? __________________

Goal # 2 (list goal)

____

Why is goal important to you? ______________________

Timeframe for completion of goal? __________________

Goal # 3 (list goal)

____

Why is goal important to you? ______________________

Timeframe for completion of goal? __________________

Use This Format to List Additional Goals on a Separate Document if Needed

Appendix 9-1—Financial Planner Checklist

Checklist For Interviewing A Financial Planner

Planner Name: ____

Company: ____

Address: ____

Phone: ____

Date: ____

1. **Do you have experience in providing advice on the topics below?**
   If yes, please indicate the number of years.

   - Retirement planning __________
   - Investment planning __________
   - Tax planning __________
   - Estate planning __________
   - Insurance planning __________
   - Integrated Planning __________
   - Other____

2. **What are your areas of expertise and how do your qualifications in those areas compare to others?**

   ____

   ____

   ____

   ____

   ____

3. **How long have you been offering financial planning advice to clients?**

   ____ Less than one year   _____ Five to 10 years
   ____ One to four years   _____ More than 10 years

4. **Briefly describe your work history:**

____

____

____

____

5. **What are your educational qualifications? Give area of study.**

____ Undergraduate Degree ______________________________
____ Advanced Degree ______________________________
____ Other ______________________________

6. **Which planning or investment management designation(s) do you hold?**

____ Certified Financial Planner or CFP®
____ Certified Funds Specialist (CFS)
____ Certified Public Accountant-Personal Financial Specialists (CPA-PFS)
____ Certified Senior Advisor (CSA)
____ Other ______________________________

7. **How many financial planning related continuing education requirements do you fulfill?**
____ hours every ______________

8. **What licenses do you hold?**

____ Insurance (Life, Health, Disability, Long Term Care)
____ Securities (NASD Series 7, 24, 63)
____ Other ______________________________

9. **A. Are you personally licensed or registered as an Investment Adviser with the:?**

____ State(s)? ____ Federal Government?
If no, why not? ______________________________

B. Is your firm licensed or registered as an Investment Adviser with the:

____ State(s)? ____ Federal Government?
If no, why not? ____________________

C. Will you provide me with your disclosure document Form ADV or its state equivalent form?

____ Yes ____ No
If No, why not? ____________________

10. What services do you offer?

____

____

11. Describe your approach to financial planning.

____

____

12. A. Who will be working with me on my plan?

Planner ____________________

Associate(s) ____________________

B. Will the same individual(s) review my financial situation?

____ Yes ____ No
If No, why not? ____________________

13. How are you paid for your services?

____ Fee ____ Fee and commission
____ Commission ____ Salary
____ Other ____________________

14. What do you typically charge?

Hourly Rate $ _______ @ hour
Flat fee (range) $ _______ to $ _________
Percentage of assets under management ________ percent

15. A. Are you employed by any company whose products or services you recommend?

____ Yes ____ No
Explain ____

B. Can you implement the plan by making transactions for us or do we have to find a properly licensed person?

____ Yes ____ No
Explain ____

C. Do professionals and sales agents to whom you may refer me to send business, fees or any other benefits to you?

____ Yes ____ No
Explain ____

D. Are you regulated by the National Association of Securities Dealers (NASD)?

____ Yes ____ No

E. Do you have oversight specifically for your insurance recommendations (i.e. licensed with the State Insurance Commissioner)?

____ Yes ____ No
Explain ____

16. Do you provide a written client engagement agreement?

____ Yes ____ No
Explain ____

References

Step 1

1. To view this report go to: www.consumerfed.org/pdfs/Financial_Planners_Study011006.pdf.
2. Federal Reserve Triennial Survey of Consumer Finances, 2004. (Note that the next update will occur at the conclusion of 2007.)

Step 2

1. U.S. Department of Labor Statistics.
2. U.S. Department of Labor compilation of job tenure experience 1983-2002.
3. *First, Break All the Rules: What the World's Greatest Managers Do Differently*, Marcus Buckingham and Curt Coffman, 1999, Simon & Schuster.
4. The Gallup Organization is world renowned for its leading work in the areas of individual and corporate development. For more information regarding The Gallup Organization's integrated services visit **www.gallup.com**.

Step 3

1. *The Millionaire Next Door*, Thomas J. Stanley, William D.Danko, Simon & Schuster Inc.
2. Federal Reserve Triennial Survey of Consumer Finances, 2004
3. Bankrate.com is a leading aggregator of financial rate information. Bankrate.com surveys approximately 5,000 financial institutions throughout the United States to get current interest rate information (www.bankrate.com).
4. Edmunds.com has been in business since 1966 producing new and used auto pricing guides, and in 1994, went online with its website, making it the first automotive online resource, www.edmunds.com.
5. www.safecareguide.com.

Step 4

1. www.bankrate.com.
2. American Consumer Credit Counseling, Inc.
3. Cambridge Consumer Credit Index.
4. Ibid.
5. SMR Research.
6. Ibid.
7. DM Review, May 2005
8. Federal Trade Commission.

Step 5

1. Social Security and Medicare Forecast: 2005, Brief Analysis 515, National Center for Policy Analysis, www.ncpa.org.
2. *Encouraging Workers to Save: The 2005 Retirement Confidence Survey* (Washington, D.C.: Employee Benefit Research Institute, 2005. EBRI Brief No. 280.
3. Ibid.
4. Internal Revenue Service, www.irs.gov.
5. Bureau of Labor Statistics.
6. Morningstar Investments, www.morningstar.com.
7. Roth 401(k) website, www.roth401k.com.
8. HSA Insider, www.hsainsider.com.
9. Ward's Dealer Business, March 1, 2004.
10. Centers for Disease Control & Prevention.
11. Blue Care Network HMO in Michigan introduced Healthy Blue Living in October 2006. This program offers enhanced benefits at no extra cost for those who follow specified steps to improve targeted health conditions.
12. www.irs.gov.
13. Ceridian, www.ceridian.com.

Step 6

1. If Series EE Bonds are purchased electronically through Treasury Direct, bonds are purchased at 100% of the bond's face value.
2. If Series I bonds are purchased electronically through Treasury Direct, the minimum purchase is $25.
3. Bond funds will often list both average maturity and duration. Average maturity will always be longer than duration when interest bearing bonds are included in the bond portfolio. Duration is shorter because it calculates the bond portfolio's average maturity and adds to it bond interest payments received from each bond in the portfolio. The net effect of periodic bond interest payments (which occurs generally twice per year for interest bearing bonds) results in the bond portfolio's duration being less than its overall maturity. Got that?

4. For a review of Standard & Poor's and Moody's rating methodologies for bonds, please visit their respective websites: www.standardandpoors.com; www.moodys.com .
5. Market capitalization is calculated by multiplying a company's current share price by the number of shares outstanding. The result gives investors an idea of how large the current market value is for the company's outstanding shares.
6. Investment Company Institute, www.ici.org.
7. For more information regarding Morningstar's mutual fund evaluation method, visit the Morningstar website at www.morningstar.com.
8. Ibbotson Associates from website on 11-23-05, www.ibbotson.com.

Step 7

1. An Employee's Guide to Health Benefits Under COBRA (including HIPAA special enrollment rules), U.S. Department of Labor, September 2004.
2. Disability Insurance, QuickQuote Financial, www.quickquote.com.
3. Health Affairs, February 2, 2005.
4. Quote from Robert Jacobs during a Medicare Part D discussion, October 2005.
5. American Association of Retired Persons, 2006, www.aarp.org.
6. Quotation provided from e-financial website on 8-6-06, www.efinancial.com.
7. For more information about A.M. Best, visit www.ambest.com.
8. O'Shaughnessy, Carol, Congressional Research Service, Long-Term Care: Who Will Care for the Aging Baby Boomers? Senate Hearing 107-106, June 28, 2001.
9. A good book on the topic of Long-Term Care is: Long-Term Care Your Financial Planning Guide, author is Phyllis Shelton; Kensington Books is the publisher, www.kensingtonbooks.com.
10. Save on Auto Insurance, Road and Travel Magazine, www.roadandtravel.com.
11. Insurance Information Institute, www.iii.org.
12. (Appendix 7-1) *Bringing Up Baby On A Budget*, Consumer Reports.org., June 2005, www.consumerreports.org.

Step 8

1. Exhibit concept provided by InCharge Education Foundation, www.mindyourfinances.com.
2. There are other IRAs available based on specific circumstances. IRS Publication 590 is an excellent source for information regarding different types of IRAs and specific rules associated with different IRAs. You can find publication 590 at the IRS website, www.irs.gov.
3. Publication 590, Internal Revenue Service.
4. IRS Publication 590.
5. Special Report: Value of Higher Education, Education Atlas, www.educationatlas.com.
6. The Current Population Survey is a joint project between the Bureau of Labor Statistics and the Bureau of the Census, www.bls.census.gov.
7. Digest of Education Statistics for the years 1958-1970 and the College Board figures for four-year private colleges for the years from 1971 to the present.
8. Chart Courtesy of FinAid, a recognized source for college financial aid, www.finaid.org.
9. The College Board, Trends in College Pricing 2008.

Step 9

1. Telephone survey of 1009 adults age 18 and over conducted by Harris Interactive for LexisNexis Martindale-Hubbell, April 22, April 25, 2004.
2. The Financial Planners Standards Council was established in 1995 in Canada to enforce the competency and ethics of financial planners who hold the internationally recognized designation of Certified Financial Planner, CFP®.
3. Certified Financial Planner Board of Board of Standards, Inc. Advisory Opinion 2003-1. Those who have the CFP® designation have completed rigorous testing in personal financial planning issues. The CFP® designation is recognized worldwide as a significant credential in the field of personal financial planning.
4. CFP®Advisory Opinion 2003-1.

Index

A

B

C

D

E

F

M

N

O

P

T

U

V

LOOKING FOR THE PERFECT GIFT?

What could be a nicer gift than helping someone with their financial health?

- If you are an employer, why not show your employees you really value them by giving each of them a copy?
- Give a copy of the book for Mother's Day or Father's Day to show your parents you really care about them.
- A copy of ***The 10 Steps To Financial Wellness*** would make a perfect holiday or birthday gift.

Order more than one copy and save!

Quantity	Original Cost	Your Cost
1	~~$17.95~~	$9.95*
2-9	~~$14.95~~	$3.95*
10-99	~~$12.50~~	$3.95*
100-999	~~$10.00~~	$3.95*
1000-2500	~~$8.75~~	$3.95*
>2500	Call	Call*
*Shipping & Handling charges will apply		

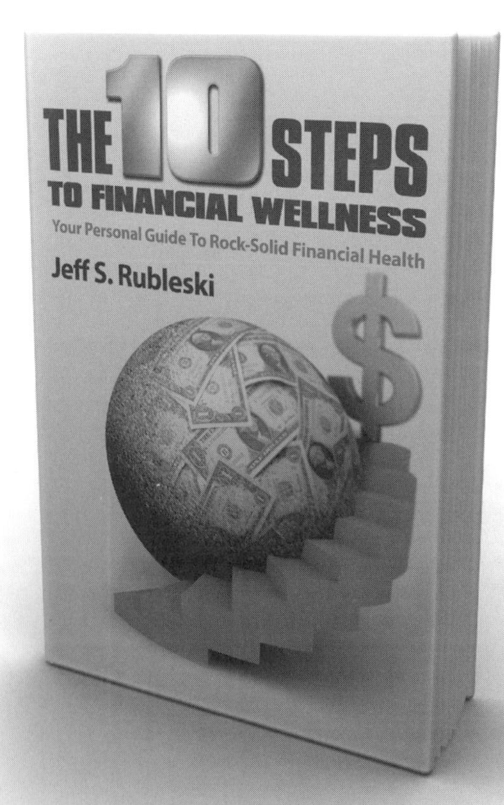

To order online visit:

www.welcoa.org

or call:

(402) 827-3590

Wellness Council of America
9802 Nicholas Street, Suite 315
Omaha, NE 68114
Phone: (402) 827-3590
Fax: (402) 827-3594
E-mail: wellworkplace@welcoa.org